THE CATASTROPHE
OF DISASTER AID

THE CATASTROPHE OF DISASTER AID

Post-2010 Earthquake Haiti, NGOs and New Vulnerabilities

Jean Max Charles

The University of the West Indies Press
Mona • St Augustine • Cave Hill • Global • Five Islands

The University of the West Indies Press
7A Gibraltar Hall Road, Mona
Kingston 7, Jamaica
www.uwipress.com

**A catalogue record of this book is available from
the National Library of Jamaica.**
978-976-640-988-3 (paperback)
978-976-640-989-0 (epub)

Cover and text design by Christina Moore Fuller
Cover photo courtesy of David Gilkey/NPR
Printed in the United States of America

Contents

List of Figures

List of Tables

Foreword by Percy C. Hintzen

Haiti's persistent vulnerability to natural disasters is the substantive ground on which this book by Jean Max Charles rests. Of critical importance is its focus on the perpetual, persistent and never-ending history of social, economic and political crises in the country. These are argued to be fundamentally important in explanations for the failure of disaster relief. The link made between "resilience" and "disaster prevention" forces us to rethink popular and official understandings that "disasters" are "natural" and "inevitable" and cannot be prevented. Failure to do so leaves communities perpetually stuck in a cycle of unending "perennial relief management" and "increasing vulnerabilities". This argument is predicated on settled understandings in the scholarly literature that "natural events" need not morph into "disasters". It guides the analytical and methodological strategies of the book and leads logically to a focus on resilience.

Jean Max Charles emphasizes the inevitable link between the capacity for resilience and the social, economic and political conditions that can prevent or mitigate the transformation of natural events into disasters. What becomes evident is that differences in vulnerabilities occur across communities. This highlights the artificiality of national boundaries. Why? As the late Haitian anthropologist Michel-Rolph Trouillot has made clear, the processes and practices that explain vulnerability exist at the very local level. In the final analysis, differences among local communities are rooted in the fraught political, economic and social history of a country and the crises that they engender. In this "age of climate change", this assertion comes with universal implications.

"Resilience" takes centre stage in the analytical framework of the book, as it should. But what is extraordinarily innovative is Charles's rejection of the notion that the application of development orthodoxy is its salvation. Indeed, such application may well exacerbate the vulnerabilities of communities to natural events. Comparative findings measured across three communities selected for ethnographic focus by Charles make this a compelling argument. The most "developed" of the three, measured in standardized terms of wealth, material amenities and infrastructure, happens to be the least resilient. The "poorest" experienced the fastest rate of recuperation and recovery and the least disruption. Charles uses this finding to make a much larger claim regarding the constitutive elements of true development.

A key argument of the book is that disaster aid can become a critical ingredient in developmental transformation. And herein lies the potential of NGOs due to their oversized role in Haiti as an effective alternative and surrogate to the failed government apparatus. Their multiple presences, with multiple forms of engagement across multiple communities, provided Charles with the opportunity for comparative analysis, out of which emerged one of the most important findings of the book: that effective resilience is predicated upon local collaboration and local involvement in disaster relief. That it demands a functioning and effective local authority. And that it requires participation by local organizations. Together, these can produce the type of developmental transformation congruent with the necessary conditions that resilience demands. The need, therefore, is for a fundamental shift in disaster relief and disaster management spending. The typical pattern of disbursement to national authorities under conditions specified, defined and imposed by transnational funders is fraught with failure.

At the most general, and perhaps the most important level, the book makes significant and critically important contributions to the multiple fields of disaster relief, development and NGO studies, and the ways that they intersect. It critically engages with orthodox economic development policies imposed universally on countries in the Global South. It argues that these policies exacerbate vulnerabilities to disaster and the crises they produce. Dr Charles uses the focus on resilience to critically engage with and challenge the orthodoxy of development theory and policy. He argues, following Nobel Laureate Amartya Sen, that development and disaster relief must rest on the enhancement of the capabilities and capacities of people at the local level. Disaster relief, he asserts, can serve as the springboard to such enhancement. In the final analysis, his argument, following Sen, is that the goal of development should be to ensure that people are entitled to live a life they believe they deserve. And when they are provided with the capacities and capabilities to do so, their vulnerabilities to natural events will be all but eliminated.

Percy C. Hintzen
Professor Emeritus, University of California, Berkeley
Former Professor of Global and Sociocultural Studies, Florida International University

Foreword by Edwin Everham III

I have worked on the ecological impacts of disturbances for over thirty years. My research has focused primarily on forests, inland and upland systems in Puerto Rico and mangrove forests in Southwest Florida, encompassing a variety of disturbance events – hurricanes, fires, volcanic eruptions, droughts, cold events, exotic invasions, human development and ecological restoration. I am interested in the dynamics of recovery, the adaptations that make some species and most ecological systems resistant and resilient to disturbances they have experienced through evolutionary times.

When Jean Max Charles joined The Water School at Florida Gulf Coast University in 2022, I was excited to share our interest in disasters and recovery, but I especially valued his expertise in human systems. He regularly teaches the seminar "Disasters and Development", an elective course, "Climate Change, Vulnerability, Adaptation, and Resilience" and one of our core courses for the environmental studies degree, "Regional Environments", with a focus on Latin America and the Caribbean. His personal experience as a Haitian brings a powerful insight and truth to his teaching and writing. Who better than a Haitian to write one of the "new narratives" about his country?

In Southwest Florida, where we both now live, our return times (the gap between events) for hurricanes have decreased from forty-four years to eleven, then to five and now to two. My work involves understanding how native systems respond to the increasing frequency of these events. As our community has been so profoundly impacted, I have become more interested in how human systems and societies rebound. Does each disturbance make us more able to handle the next, or does each destructive event lower our resilience? Losing the roof of my house to Hurricane Irma certainly refocused the issue for me.

Jean and I first had an opportunity to share our complementary expertise on a panel, "Crisis Management and Disaster Response", as part of the Third Annual Hanseatic League of Universities Conference. The conference theme was "Vectors of Resilience". Jean's focus on the social impacts and responses to hurricanes and the 2010 earthquake in Haiti was enlightening. I continue to learn from him about parallel and divergent processes toward resistance and resilience in human communities versus other ecological systems. I was first attracted to disturbance ecology with the hope that natural systems could teach us how to manage human systems more effectively. Jean, through this book, continues my education.

Before reading his book, I would have confidently stated that human action does not create earthquake disasters; that there is not a human component to earthquake disturbance – independent of hydraulic fracking – as there is in flooding and wildfires. It is clear that floods and fires are directly linked to human actions, which create conditions that make these disturbances more frequent and intense. Increasingly, we are experiencing the "wicked problem" of climate change, which indirectly creates conditions that lead to more frequent flooding, more intense fires and stronger hurricanes. However, Jean taught me that humans turn disturbances into disasters by creating vulnerable systems and failing to build resistance and resilience. We do not make earthquakes more intense; we make their impacts more destructive. Thus, this book's title.

Jean's phrase "unending relief" highlights the often incomplete response of NGOs in Haiti and arguably across the developing world. It is a particularly poignant reality in disaster response. If the societal response to an earthquake, a hurricane or a catastrophic fire is exclusively "relief" – if all we do is strive to get back to where we were – we are stuck in an endless cycle of disaster and reactive emergency response. We "build it back" but miss the opportunity to "build it back better".

Jean makes the case that "the essential problem of Haiti is that the state is destroying the nation". Although he cautions us about applying his conclusions to the developed world, it is clear to me that his focus on recovery from earthquake impacts in Haiti speaks more broadly to disturbance across the globe. Our social, economic and political systems may also be "destroying" our human existence as we continue to respond to climate change and the myriad cascading disturbances reactively rather than proactively, ignoring the underlying systemic context. There is much we can learn from this study of the earthquake in Haiti and much that this book can teach us all.

Jean ends his Preface with:

What Haiti needs now is leaders who are capable of envisioning and creating a new narrative, a new négritude and a new nation to help the country reach its true potential.

Don't we all?

Edwin "Win" Everham III
Disturbance Ecologist and co-editor of Making the Sustainable University
Professor of Ecology and Environmental Studies
Florida Gulf Coast University

Preface

Doing Research Amid Unrest: Negotiating My Role and My Positionality

I moved to the United States from Haiti in 2003 at a time when Haiti State University students were embroiled in a campaign against what they claimed was President Jean Bertrand Aristide's attempt to impose a new form of dictatorship in Haiti. The social and economic conditions in Haiti were already bad when I left the country. However, when I returned fifteen years later to conduct my fieldwork for my dissertation, I found a country in complete disarray, plunged into abject misery and crippled by violence. However, within that same country, I saw others living luxurious lives, protected behind security gates and driving bulletproof vehicles.

I began my fieldwork in August 2018. Just a month before, on 6–7 July, after Jovenel Moïse's administration had announced a gasoline price hike of 38 per cent, a 47 per cent increase for diesel and violent riots had erupted in Port-au-Prince. After two days of massive violent protests, the government rescinded the decision, and the country regained its calm. However, this calm did not last long. A new crisis, the crisis of PetroCaribe, surfaced in August, plunged the country into chaos. The PetroCaribe crisis was started by a tweet from Gilbert Mirambeau Jr, a Haitian filmmaker living in Montreal, Canada, on 14 August 2018. Gilbert Mirambeau Jr posted a picture of himself on Twitter, blindfolded and asking, *"kot kob petwo karibe a"* (Where is the PetroCaribe money?) The tweet went viral, and the riots erupted again.

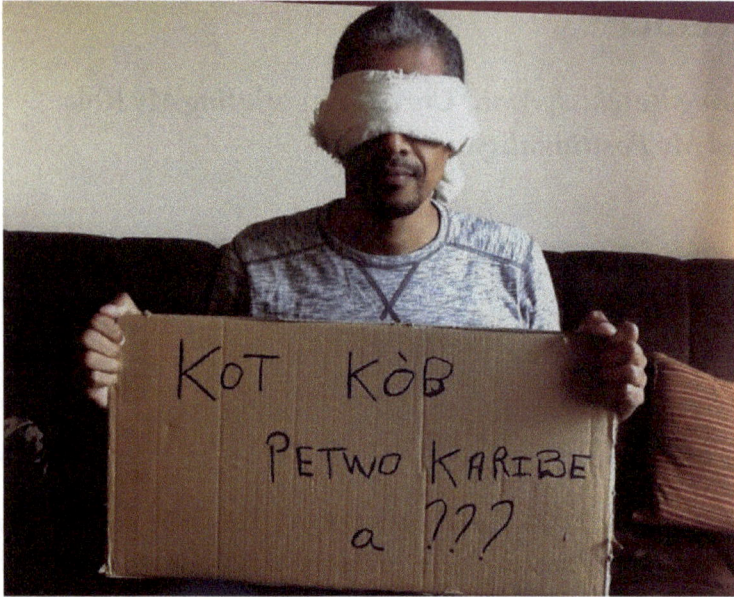

Gilbert Mirambeau Jr, posted on Twitter "Kot kob Petwo Karibe a? English translation: Where is the PetroCaribe money? Posted on 14 August 2018.

PetroCaribe was an agreement initiated by Hugo Chavez, the Venezuelan president at the time, with other countries in the Caribbean and Latin America. The agreement was aimed at building social, economic and political integrations of the countries in Latin America and the Caribbean. It was intended to provide oil at concessionary prices to Caribbean countries. According to the agreement, the member nations purchasing oil from Venezuela would pay a concessionary price. They could pay 5–50 per cent of the price of oil market value up front. The remainder would be paid through a seventeen- to twenty-five-year financing with a 1–2 per cent interest annually (Cederlöf, Gustav and Kingsbury 2019). Haiti signed the PetroCaribe agreement in 2006. In the case of Haiti, under the agreement, the Haitian government would pay 60 per cent of the oil price up front, while 40 per cent was supposed to be used for the economic development of the country and to fund social programmes. In 2018, the country was expected to have nearly $2 billion in savings from the PetroCaribe fund. However, the money went missing (Time 2019; BMPD 2019).[1]

The dilapidation of the PetroCaribe funds that Mirambeau was attempting to denounce underscores the pervasive reality of corruption in the country. The history of Haiti is engrained with corruption and mismanagement of public funds. This history of corruption can be traced back to the early years following independence in 1804, but it has been worsening since the end of the American occupation of Haiti. A Haitian adage says that "stealing from the state is not stealing" as a justification for stealing from the state. Many reports from the World Bank during the 1990s and 2000s described Haiti as a predatory state, where the government and the elites use the state resources for individual enrichment. The 2018 Amnesty International Index on corruption ranked Haiti as the second most corrupt country in the hemisphere.[2]

President Jovenel Moïse took office in February 2017. Multiple reports alleged that he participated in the embezzlement of the PetroCaribe fund before he came to office, during the time he led the company Agritrans. This company was paid around US$700,000 to repair some roads; the roads were never repaired (Time 2019).[3] As a result, waves of anti-corruption demonstrators occupied the streets, put the country under gridlock and demanded the removal of President Jovenel Moïse and the trial of people complicit in squandering the PetroCaribe fund. The gridlock produced by these crises has been a pervasive feature of Haiti, contributing to the worsening of social and economic conditions. I returned to the country in November 2019 as a Fulbright Scholar still amid unrest, violent protests, territories under the control of gangs and an economy asphyxiating as the inflation rate soared to 30 per cent.

Conducting research in such a complex social and political environment proved to be a daunting task. Drawing from my experiences of being born and raised in Haiti, and with the help of friends and connections, I was able to navigate unsafe areas of Port-au-Prince to meet with community organization leaders and NGO beneficiaries despite the challenges. The most challenging obstacles, however, came in interactions with local political leaders and government officials. I was often treated as an outsider and Haitian American researcher with undisclosed missions. Therefore, some government officials felt uncomfortable talking to me. Being aware of positionality and how this mistrust may impact the way the respondents convey information, I exerted much patience to clearly explain my research objectives, build trust with my informants and gather the data that I needed without compromising the validity of my research.

Due to the sensitive nature of this research, I have chosen not to disclose the names of my informants or include any identifiable details that could lead to their identification. I use pseudonyms for most of my informants unless they have explicitly authorized me to use their real names. The university professors I interviewed as experts granted me that authorization. The names of the experts mentioned in this book, hence, refer to their real names.

The Need for a New Narrative

Scholars have been stressing the need for new narratives about Haiti (Ulysse 2005; Singh and Barton-Dock 2015). Haiti is widely recognized as the poorest country in the Western Hemisphere, but it has not always been the case. Heinl and Heinl (2005) report that, during the 1930s, US ambassadors in the Dominican Republic used to stay in Haiti but travelled to the Dominican Republic to hold office hours, as conditions in Haiti were better than in the neighbouring country. Following the end of the US occupation from 1934 until 1957, the country experienced some growth. However, one can argue that conditions of racial inequality, corruption, class domination and autocratic governance persisted, even if it was a period of growth. Yet, during that period, and even in the sixties, Haiti was one of the primary destinations for tourists in the Caribbean.

Also, during that period, the Haitian elites, notably the Black intellectual elites and the middle class, promoted a political philosophy that encouraged a valorization of the Black race. This philosophy, known as *négritude* (English: noirism), was a political philosophy that proclaimed the self-affirmation of the Black race and the values of Black people everywhere.[4] It was mainly francophone intellectuals who developed *négritude* during the 1930s to raise and cultivate a Black consciousness. Some leading figures of *négritude* are Jean Price-Mars (Haiti), Aimé Césaire (Martinique), Léopold Sédar Senghor[5] (Senegal) and Léon Damas (French Guiana), and to a certain extent Frantz Fanon

(Martinique). While *négritude* can be considered an international movement, it began in Haiti. Aimé Césaire usually referred to Haiti as the country where '*négritude*' arose for the first time (Nwankwo 2008; Beslin 2008). That philosophy mobilized the Black elites to political and nationalist ends.

The root of *négritude* can be traced to Antenor Firmin's book, *The Equality of Human Races*. However, the development of the philosophy can be credited to Jean-Price Mars. Antenor Firmin planted the seed, and Jean Price-Mars watered the plant and made it grow. Price-Mars, who was one of Haiti's most prolific intellectuals, sang Firmin's praises for sharpening the glorious work of the rehabilitation of the Black race in the twentieth century (Charles 2020). In Senegal, the *négritude* helped to guide the country into independence with pride. The *négritude* theorist Léopold Sédar Senghor became the first president of Senegal in 1960.

Before even Senghor became president, the Black elites in Haiti employed *négritude* for the conquest of political power. Nevertheless, throughout the American occupation and until 1946, every Haitian president was mulatto, or of mixed Black and White ancestry. Léon Dumarsais Estimé became the first Black president of Haiti in 1946 and nominated Jean-Price Mars to serve in his cabinet. Estimé pursued national development policies. Under his government, Haiti became the first destination for tourism in the Caribbean and Port-au-Prince became a modern capital, one of the most beautiful in the region. The priority for the people in the government was mainly the public good and the construction of a Black nation as a reference to the world, not individual interests in the pursuit of wealth. Yet, one can argue that the regime of Estimé was still plagued with some level of corruption, debt and mismanagement. However, his regime was much better than what followed. Magloire, a Black general, ousted Estimé in 1950. He led a very corrupt regime that was dependent on American support and prepared the groundwork for Francois Duvalier.

The decline of the country began under the Duvalier state.[6] It reached its zenith after 1986.[7] In order to grasp the complete picture of the current events in Haiti, it is essential to understand the events and attitudes of the 1980s. The fall of Duvalier led to extreme violence in Haiti. The Haitian people wanted to uproot all the symbols of the regime and exterminate all the partisans of Duvalier, particularly the *Tontons macoutes*, which was the paramilitary force Duvalier used to impose violence and fear among Haitians. To do so, the Haitian people utilized extreme methods of violence. It was a time of extreme revenge against Duvalier and his partisans. By doing so, the generation of the 1980s was socialized into a new philosophy of widespread violence, uprising, riots and killing of political enemies and partisans of the regime who trespassed. They learned that the only way to resolve political issues and disagreements was violence. The generation that grew up in the 1980s is now the political leaders of the country. Perhaps because they are accustomed to the political philosophies of violence, deep-seated mistrust and division, it appears they are replicating, probably unconsciously, the strategies they learned during the 1980s.

However, one can argue, here again, that political instability and widespread violence have been a pervasive feature of post-revolutionary Haiti. Nevertheless, the American occupation of Haiti from 1915 through 1934 brought a long period of stability, which continued for the most part throughout the Duvalier regime. There was a possibility of turning the 2010 earthquake disaster into an opportunity for a whole renewal of the country, but the Haitian elites failed. During the last few years, Haiti has been in complete disarray. President Jovenel Moïse was assassinated on 7 July 2021. Since then, Haiti's security has remained dire, with gangs reportedly controlling over 80 per cent of the capital (Wilson Center 2023). Gang violence and kidnappings have reached unprecedented levels, displacing hundreds of thousands of people and prompting a significant number of Haitians to attempt to leave the country (Wilson Center 2023).

The elites cannot find a compromise to save the nation, the state has become even weaker and local gangs are terrorizing the population. What Haiti needs now are leaders capable of envisioning and creating a new narrative, a new *négritude* and a new nation to help the country reach its true potential.

Acknowledgements

This book emerged from my dissertation research in Haiti, which the Fulbright Scholar Program funded. I am grateful to the Fulbright US Scholar Program for selecting me as a Fulbright Scholar for Haiti (2019–20). This grant helped me tremendously as I completed the dissertation. I want to express my sincere gratitude to my dissertation advisor, Professor Percy Hintzen. It has especially been a privilege for me to work under his guidance. Professor Bidegain offered relevant comments on the research project, and I am eternally thankful for her input.

I owe an outstanding debt of gratitude to Rosalie Schurman, my doctorate classmate. She worked on the project from its inception. She offered many important comments and helped me to refine the work. I am also grateful to Mckenna Clarke, my friends Nadège Joassaint-Meyer and Jude Lesperance, my former students Judith Juste and Rachel Pavel, who diligently worked to refine the final document. Thanks to Maria Barbero, also my doctorate classmate, for her advice and suggestions. I also want to thank the team who surveyed Haiti. I am especially indebted to Abnel Désamours and Pierre Anthony Garraud. The survey could not have been possible without the support, guidance and expertise of Dr Qing Lai, to whom I will be forever grateful. A special thanks to all my interviewees, the community organizations and the NGOs who welcomed me and shared with me a wealth of information.

I am also indebted to all my family and friends who supported me throughout this project, especially my mother, Martha, my brothers, Pèdre, Edward, Woody and Hémeck, and my dear friend Oliver Thompson. My wife Emilie and my two sons, Max and Berkley, have been extraordinary sources of encouragement. Their support made this book possible. They have my love and my sincere thanks.

Acronyms and Abbreviations

ALNAP	Active Learning Network for Accountability and Performance in Human Action
BRAC	Bangladesh Rural Advancement Committee
CCRIF	Caribbean Catastrophe Risk Insurance Facility
CIDA	Canadian International Development Agency
CARE	Cooperative for American Relief Everywhere
CRS	Catholic Relief Service
COOPI	Cooperazione Internationale
CNSA	National Coordination of Food Security
DRR	Disaster Risk Reduction
EERP	Emergency Economic Recovery Program
ECHO	European Commission Humanitarian Aid
ECVMAS	Enquêtes sur les Conditions de Vie des Ménages Après le Séisme (Surveys on the Living Conditions of Households After the Earthquake)
EERP	Economic Recovery Program
EPI	Expanded Program on Immunization
EU	European Union
FAO	Fund and Agriculture Organization of the United States
FUNCOL	Foundation of Colombian Communities
GDP	Gross Domestic Product
GOH	Government of Haiti
HISI	Haitian Institute of Statistics and Informatics
IDB	International Development Bank

IFS	International Financial Institutions
IMF	International Monetary Funds
INGO	International Non-governmental Organizations
INS	Immigration and Naturalization Service
ISDR	International Strategy for Disaster Reduction
IPCC	Intergovernmental Panel on Climate Change
KRIFAH	Kri Fanm
LRRD	Linking Relief, Rehabilitation and Development
NGO	Non-governmental Organizations
OCHA	Office for the Coordination of Humanitarian Affairs
ODSETAD	Organization for Development and Technical Support for Haitian Artisans
OECD	Organization for Economic Cooperation and Development
OFDA	Office of the United States Foreign Disaster Assistance
OSGSA	Office of the Secretary General's Special Advisor
RFPC	Group Professional Women in Construction
SAP	Structural Adjustment Policy
SDG	Sustainable Development Goals
UN	United Nations
UNDP	United Nations Development Program
UNFPA	United Nations Population Fund
UNICEF	United Nations Children's Funds
USAID	United States Agency for International Development
VWH	Voice of Women in Haiti

ONE

Haiti: Underdevelopment and the Vulnerability to Natural Disasters

Misfortune is never invited. And it comes and sits at the table without permission, and it eats, leaving nothing but bones.

Jacques Roumain, prominent Haitian writer, and cultural anthropologist.

In January 2010, a massive 7.0 magnitude earthquake struck Haiti. According to the Haitian government, more than 220,000 people lost their lives, 300,000 were injured and 1.3 million became homeless (GOH 2010). The earthquake also severely damaged the country's infrastructure; an estimated 60 per cent of the country's public services were destroyed, including 80 per cent of schools and 50 per cent of hospitals (GOH 2010). In the wake of the earthquake, there was an outpouring of global support as the international community immediately assisted the devastated country. At the International Donors Conference Toward a New Future for Haiti, held two months after the catastrophe, donors pledged US$9 billion for the country's recovery and reconstruction (UN 2010). The Haitian government, known for its ineffectiveness, was excluded from access to and management of these funds (Pierre-Louis 2012; Zanotti 2011). Thus, the money was disbursed directly to NGOs.

The decision to disburse relief and reconstruction aid through NGOs proved ineffective. A decade after the earthquake, Haiti is still struggling desperately. According to a household survey (ECVMAS 2012), about two-thirds of Haitians live under the national poverty line, earning a daily income of less than US$2.40, and 25 per cent live under the national extreme poverty line of US$1.23 per day. The secretary-general's 2017 report on the United Nations Stabilization Mission in Haiti stressed that 2.35 million (of 10.4 million) people in Haiti needed immediate assistance, while more than 143,110 are estimated to be suffering from acute malnutrition. The World Bank reported in 2017 that Haiti is still vulnerable to natural disasters, with more than 90 per cent of the population at risk.

Yet the World Bank has reported modest improvements in the social and economic conditions in Haiti in the first few years following the earthquake (Singh and Barton-Dock 2015; The World Bank 2015).[1] According to the World Bank, poverty declined from 31 per cent to 24 per cent between 2000 and 2012. Extreme poverty also fell from 21 per cent to 12 per cent in urban areas. However, findings indicate that this improvement was largely a result of increased remittances from abroad, which augmented from 42 per cent in 2000 to 69 per cent in 2012. Also, income inequality has remained stagnant since 2001. The richest 20 per cent are still earning more than 64 per cent of the total income of the country (Hintzen 2019; Singh and Barton-Dock 2015).

Given the poor results of Haiti's post-disaster aid, it is clear that disaster aid does not always produce positive outcomes and long-term transformation. Numerous scholars (Anderson and Woodrow 1989; Delica-Willison and Willison 2004; Hilhorst and Bankoff 2004) have argued that even well-intentioned relief can create unforeseen vulnerabilities and make socio-economic conditions even worse.

The above argument leads to the central thesis of this book: to produce long-term outcomes, disaster aid and relief must make development a centrepiece of its intervention in order to reduce future vulnerability and build resilient communities. Also, key to this book is an examination of the extent to which disaster resilience was built into the post-quake NGO-provided relief in Haiti. In this way, I investigate both the effectiveness and the limitations of NGO aid regarding efforts to provide sustainable development outcomes in the wake of disasters. Using Haiti as a case study, I aim to examine how the billions of dollars in disaster aid, provided through NGOs for relief and reconstruction following the 2010 magnitude 7.0 earthquake, can be more effectively delivered and managed. The focus is on identifying strategies to ensure long-term results and reduce the risk of future disasters in a nation as underdeveloped and disaster-prone as Haiti.

Haiti's Vulnerability to Natural Disasters

According to the World Bank report *Haiti: Toward a New Narrative* (Singh and Barton-Dock 2015):

> The Haitian population is one of the most exposed in the world to natural disasters: hurricanes, floods, and earthquakes. Haiti has a higher number of disasters per km² than the average of the Caribbean countries... disasters tend to affect disproportionately the poorest and the marginal populations settling in flood zones and coastal areas, in particular in the case of tropical storms where almost 50 per cent of damages and losses to the productive sectors have been concentrated in the agricultural sector. (Singh and Barton-Dock 2015, 21)

Among the Caribbean countries, Haiti is the most vulnerable to disasters. The losses and damages resulting from natural disasters in Haiti are far greater than those in many of the other Caribbean countries. From 1971 to 2014, Haiti experienced 137 natural disasters (the 2010 earthquake excluded), which resulted in 23,427 deaths and an average GDP loss of 1.776 per cent (Singh and Barton-Dock 2015, 22). During that same period, there were fewer casualties due to natural disasters in the Dominican Republic, Jamaica, Nicaragua, Honduras, El Salvador, Guatemala, Costa Rica and Panama combined (EM-DAT 2018). Haiti's high vulnerability to natural disasters is not, however, inherent to the country's geography – it is not an intrinsic feature of its natural and geographical conditions. Thus, it is imperative to compare Haiti and the Dominican Republic since the two countries share the same island. Haiti had twice as many natural disasters from 1971 to 2014 as the Dominican Republic. According to the World Bank, Haiti's greater vulnerability to disasters is reflected in the consequences of these events (deforestation, floods, etc.) in terms of both human and economic losses. These reflect the inadequacy of drainage, large populations settling in flood zones and the lack of sound building codes (Singh and Barton-Dock 2015, 22).

While this argument is justified, I argue that the high vulnerability must be analysed in a broader political-economic context. It carries with it the legacy of the past and the internal conflicts that pervasively marked the nation, but mostly, it is a result of failed neoliberal development policies implemented in Haiti in the 1980s (Dupuy 1997, 2005; Schuller 2009, 2012).

International Factors: The Legacy of the Past

After Haiti's independence in 1804, which created the first Black independent nation in the Western Hemisphere, the country was politically and economically isolated. In the year following the Haitian Revolution, France – with the help of the United States and allied European powers – orchestrated a diplomatic isolation of the new Black Republic (Farmer 2006). The country's independence produced such a fear of revolutionary contagion that White colonizers in Europe and the United States felt compelled to act to avoid potential replication. As a result, Haiti was ostracized and isolated for most of the nineteenth century, which had serious and long-lasting economic consequences for the young nation.

> This isolation was imposed on Haiti by a frightened white world, and Haiti became a test case, first, for those arguing about emancipation and then, after the end of slavery, for those arguing about the capacity of blacks for self-government. Great Britain was one of the few nations that had diplomatic relations with Haiti, and it was from the writings of English racists and abolitionists that Haiti began to garner widespread bad press. (Lawless 1992, 56)

In addition to the international racial conspiracy against Haiti, in 1825, France imposed a heavy indemnity on the country. This was to compensate for the financial loss French colonizers encountered during the revolution. Afraid of an eventual French power grab, the Haitian government agreed to pay this indemnity. It took Haiti almost the entire nineteenth century to pay the "independence debt", which consequently led to the country's bankruptcy. However, it would be disingenuous to attribute Haiti's overall vulnerability toward natural disasters to international causes. National factors, combined with local factors in Port-au-Prince, played critical roles in the 2010 earthquake.

Internal Conflicts and Underdevelopment

Internal conflicts also contribute to Haiti's struggles. The Haitian Revolution was possible due to an alliance between Blacks and mulattoes. This alliance was inherently fragile, as the mulattoes had a vested interest in preserving slavery. After their revolutionary success, the two factions began to fight for control of the new nation. The issue of the colour line has thus augmented deep-seated divisions and class struggles in the country for centuries. Furthermore, Haiti, as the first Black independent nation, lacked a prior example on which to build. Mobilizing a populace accustomed to slavery proved a formidable task for the country's initial leaders. Consequently, over two hundred years after the revolution, Haiti continues to grapple with the lingering effects of slavery and colonization.

Deep-seated social divisions and political instability have undermined the country's capacity to build a nation. If a nation is perceived as an "imagined community", a socially constructed community imagined by people who view themselves as part of the same group, notwithstanding they may never know each other (Anderson 1983, 6–7) – then Haiti, as a nation, was never fully "imagined". Instead, Haiti is a state that operates under a mechanism where political power is a means to gain wealth, and the state serves the egoistic interests of a few. The country's fundamental problem is that the state is against the nation (Trouillot 2020).

While I will analyse this premise at length in chapter 4, I must remark here that Haiti has been continually ranked among the most corrupt countries in the world by the International Corruption Index. Successive World Bank reports have attributed the causes of underdevelopment in Haiti to poor governance, political instability, long-lasting corruption and the misuse of public funds (Dupuy 1997, 2005). Particularly, the Bank's 1996 report said:

> Haiti has never had a tradition of governance aimed at providing services to the population or creating an environment conducive to sustainable growth. Instead, a small elite has supported a 'predatory state' that makes only negligible investments in human resources and basic infrastructure. (World Bank 2002, 3)

The economic elite in Haiti is composed of a few families who have dominated the country's economy for the last fifty years. With the complicity of the state and through phoney contracts, they control the ports and other important segments of the economy. This has resulted in the monopoly of key industries, distorted competition and twisted business practices (Singh and Barton-Dock 2015). Basic needs and "most important food products in the Haitian consumption basket are sold in concentrated markets, and a preliminary analysis indicates that the prices of these products are on average about 30–60 per cent higher in Haiti than in other countries from the region" (Singh and Barton-Dock 2015, 2).

The elite's economic control is entangled with the control of the state. They bribe political leaders and government officials. In return, they receive economic advantages, lucrative government contracts, preferential treatment and access to diverse financial and economic benefits. This quid pro quo culture is so prevalent in Haiti that the provision of government jobs has become one of the most lucrative endeavours in the country. A high position in government is the quickest and easiest way to gain access to the wealthy and to get rich through selling services and squandering public funds. An old Haitian proverb says, "stealing from the state is not stealing". As a result, the country produces more millionaires per capita than any other country in the Western region (Ferguson 1999; Jean-Baptiste 2021). As a minority of the population is getting rich through political corruption and non-transparent business practices, the vast majority live in deplorable conditions.

In the years preceding the 2010 earthquake, 76 per cent of the population (more than 4.4 million people) were living on less than US$2 per day, and 56 per cent fell below the extreme poverty line of less than US$1 per day. At that time, 80 per cent of the population earned only 32 per cent of the country's income, only 30 per cent of public healthcare services were provided by the government, and 72 per cent of the population barely had access to healthcare (International Crisis Group 2009). Less than two years before the disastrous earthquake, in August and September of 2008, four tropical storms and hurricanes hit the country. Eight hundred people were killed, and nearly one million were affected, with extensive damage to the infrastructure and agriculture. This, in turn, exacerbated food shortages, increased the cost of living and caused widespread disruption and suffering (International Crisis Group 2009). While those conditions portray the profiles of the entire country in the period preceding the earthquake, the situation in Port-au-Prince was even more dire due to the high population density of the city and the unplanned growth that it had experienced during the two decades prior to the earthquake.

The Case of Port-au-Prince: Population Density and Unplanned Growth

Port-au-Prince has a long history of naturally catalysed disasters that began during the colonial period. In 1751, two years after Port-au-Prince was founded, two cyclones and two earthquakes hit Port-au-Prince. These events destroyed most of the city's buildings. In November 1770, the city was hit by one of the strongest earthquakes in the island's history. The earthquake produced a tsunami that levelled the capital, causing two hundred deaths. J. Scherer (1912), in *Great Earthquakes in the Island of Haiti*, attributes the relatively low death toll to a rumbling sound that preceded the quake, which allowed people enough time to flee their houses before the shaking started. The earthquake struck twice within four minutes. In its wake, an ordinance was passed to ban structures deemed vulnerable to natural disasters (Joseph 2008; O'Loughlin and Lander 2003).

Throughout the nineteenth and twentieth centuries, different forms of catastrophes have hit Port-au-Prince, many of which caused severe damage and human casualties. In addition to earthquakes, the most common natural disasters are cyclones, tropical storms and floods. However, over the last thirty years, Port-au-Prince's vulnerability to natural disasters has seemed to increase. For example, the low death toll in 1770 was attributed to a public understanding of tsunami warning signs, a low population density and the sturdy way homes were constructed. It also seems that the government was able to implement effective measures, such as the ordinance for the construction of low-risk homes.

This is no longer the case. To understand Port-au-Prince's current high vulnerability to natural disasters, we first need to situate the city within the larger context of a country with a past that is inextricably entangled with external hostilities, organized international racial conspiracy and long-lasting political instability, as I demonstrated earlier. Secondly, we must analyse the local factors that contribute to Port-au-Prince's vulnerability, particularly internal migration and unplanned growth.

Compared to Port-au-Prince, rural areas have always been neglected, and thus, economic and social conditions were even more grim in rural areas. Migration to urban spaces, particularly Port-au-Prince, constituted the only way out for abandoned peasants; thirteen thousand people from rural areas migrated annually to Port-au-Prince, swelling the city's slums (World Bank 1998). In 1982, the population in Port-au-Prince was estimated to be 720,000 (World Bank 1998); in 2009, it reached 2.3 million, which represented a density of 65,000 people per square mile (World Population 2020).

With the massive migration to Port-au-Prince, the quality of urban life has significantly deteriorated. As the World Bank states, "the rapid and unplanned growth of the low-income population in urban areas has created high-density settlements and exerted extreme pressure on the scarce basic services and limited infrastructure of the cities" (World Bank 1998, 9). Road conditions worsened, and the already-limited drainage canals filled with waste, and garbage increased the occurrence of floods. In addition, construction in unsafe zones became normal. With a state that enforces no building codes or public safety laws, people have built unsafe structures and now live in unsanitary, overcrowded and dangerous conditions. Such conditions render Port-au-Prince extremely vulnerable to catastrophic natural disasters, and this explains the massive damages resulting from the January 2010 earthquake.

People from the rural areas in Haiti have been migrating to Port-au-Prince since the US occupation of Haiti. In effect, one of the pervasive consequences of the US occupation in Haiti was the centrality of the government in Port-au-Prince that it provoked (Athur 2003; Trouillot 2000; Charles 2002). All the government's offices were in Port-au-Prince. The university, schools and hospitals were all located in Port-au-

Prince. People often went to Port-au-Prince to get services unavailable anywhere else in the country. Some of them did not come back to their town or countryside but stayed in the capital. Nevertheless, the massive migration towards Port-au-Prince during the three decades prior to the earthquake was primarily the consequence of a specific political-economic policy: neoliberalism.

Neoliberalism began in Haiti in the 1980s, creating a massive disruption in the country's social, economic and demographic conditions. It also created conditions that favoured the high population density and unplanned growth in Port-au-Prince prior to the earthquake, which consequently rendered the city vulnerable to natural disasters. In chapter 3, I will discuss broadly how the neoliberal policy was implemented in Haiti. However, it is essential to briefly analyse neoliberalism and some of its normal political and economic implications.

Neoliberalism: A Brief Analysis

Neoliberalism, as a development model, involves the restructuring of domestic economies to expand their markets. It rests on the assumptions of neoclassical economics, which eclipsed the interventionist state model (Ferguson 2006; Robinson 2014). Neoliberalism de-emphasizes the social goals of national development while emphasizing participation in the world economy through tariff reduction, export promotion, financial deregulation and relaxation of foreign investment rules (McMichael 2008). These policies reformulate development to a global project. Neoliberal ideas may be traced from the beginning of the twentieth century through Karl Polanyi's analysis of the free market mechanism (Polanyi 1957). However, neoliberal ideas were adopted in the wake of classical economic theorists such as Adam Smith and David Ricardo. It was through economists such as Milton Friedman and Gary Berker that neoliberal ideas became fully articulated in the 1960s as a dominant economic school of thought. Politically, neoliberalism came to the forefront of Western economic doctrine through Ronald Reagan and Margaret Thatcher in the 1980s. Both leaders saw the government as an obstacle to economic freedom, not a solution. Thatcher in England and Reagan in the United States attacked what they called "big government" and the welfare state. Their policies focused on restructuring public sector activities by increasing the role of corporations and the private sector in order to achieve greater economic efficiency (Ong 1999, 2006).

In the 1980s, neoliberalism began to be exported to the Third World as a set of instruments for development. Neoliberal policies were collectively referenced as the Washington Consensus, a term first used in 1989 by the economist John Williamson "to refer to the policy reforms imposed when debtor countries in Latin America were called on to 'set their houses in order' and submit to strong conditionality" (Peet and Hartwick 2009, 84). Those policy reforms mainly included: 1) fiscal discipline, 2) reducing public expenditures, 3) tax reform, 4) financial liberalization, 5) unified and competitive exchange rates, 6) trade liberalization, 7) openness to direct foreign investment, 8) privatization, 9) deregulation and 10) secure property rights (Peet and Hartwick 2009, 95). The policies were intended to be used as conditions for lending money to Third World countries. The International Financial Institutions (IFIs) applied neoliberal policies under the appellation of "structural adjustment reforms".

Structural adjustment, then, describes a package of policies associated with loans to developing countries by the International Monetary Fund (IMF), the World Bank, donor governments and regional financial institutions. It consists of policies and practices directed toward the control of inflation (stabilization), a reduction of government intervention in favour of the market (liberalization), and the privatization of the public sector institutions to "improve the technical efficiency of production" (Clark 1991; Escobar 1995; Goldin 2016). Based on its conditions, a state adopting such reforms would be compelled to limit its involvement in national state-centred economic development, cease or reduce its regulatory intervention in the private sector and considerably reduce social entitlements as well as healthcare and education expenditures (Degnbol-Martinussen and Enberg-Pedersen 2005; Dupuy 2005; Goldin 2016).

These structural adjustment policies have led to increased corporate profitability. Debt service payments on loans with high interest rates in the early 1980s contributed to several years of record earnings for international banks (Rahnema and Bawtree 1997). However, the social and economic costs of debt-servicing regimes on the population of the Third World proved to be disastrous. The structural adjustment programmes were associated with high unemployment rates while driving up the cost of essential goods and services. As Arturo Escobar points out, "the burden of Structural Adjustment policies, although affecting drastically the middle and popular classes as a whole, has fallen harder on the poor, especially the poor women" (1995, 176). The repercussions were evident in the creation of conditions that led to the Third World's reliance on NGOs, and they completely altered the architecture of power and governance in countries pursuing neoliberal programmes.

Neoliberal Policies, NGOs and the Implications on the State

The term "NGO" emerged in 1945, in the immediate post-war period, when the newly formed United Nations granted private international organizations a consultative status to the UN Economic and Social Council (ECOSOC) (Willetts 2011; Reimann 2006). Article 71 of the UN charter stipulates, "The Economic and Social Council may make suitable arrangements for consultation with non-governmental organizations which are concerned with matters within its competence." In the early years, NGOs were understood as voluntary organizations, private, not-for-profit and independent of state control (Willetts 2011; Torpey-Saboe 2015). They were the continuity of a movement that sprouted during World War II when voluntary organizations began to aid war soldiers and provide food and supplies to communities in Europe affected by the war. Later, NGOs became recognized as a part of civil society. Civil society is often seen, particularly in the West, as a distinct entity, separate from the state and the market forces (Bebbington et al. 2008; Della Porta and Diani 2011; Stiles 2008). It encompasses the "organized" groups of society working for the people's interests and promoting their will. It includes churches, unions and other groups of the private sphere that coalesce together with the conscious goal of challenging the status quo and providing solutions to various societal issues (Lewis 2002; Sternberg 2010).

This separation between the state and civil society is, however, a staunch departure from Antonio Gramsci's account of civil society. In effect, Gramsci, the most influential theorist of civil society, viewed civil society as an integral part of the state and its most resilient feature (Boothman 2015; Buttigieg 1995, 2005). In Gramsci's account, this relationship between the state and civil society is maintained through the condition of hegemony that the ruling class imposes on the rest of the population (Buttigieg 1995; Eagleton 2013; Heywood 1994). Hegemony is not coercive. It is achieved by popular consent, through which the ruling class often wins over possible hostile subaltern groups by tactically making their interests look like those of the popular class (Charles 2021).

We have seen this form of hegemony take root in Europe, particularly with the rise of fascism. However, this was not the case in Latin America and the Caribbean, where several countries in that region were ruled by ruthless dictators. Indeed, during the 1960s and 1970s, Latin America was known for its human rights violations, injustice, extreme poverty and public corruption. The development state that promoted the betterment of the people in the region did not bear much fruit (Peet and Hartwick 2009; DAC 1995; Stiles 1998). Instead, massive hunger and social and economic injustices had riddled many Latin American countries. Those conditions created a fertile terrain for the emergence of liberation theology. Latin American theologian proponents of liberation theology, such as Gustavo Gutiérrez, Leonardo Boff and Jon Sobrino[2] emphasized a theology that liberates the poor and the oppressed and promotes economic equality. As an alternative to the state's inability to meet the people's needs, NGOs became an important vehicle to achieve alternative development goals (Penada 2013). During the 1960s and 1970s, many NGOs were born out of the church. As the church constitutes a vital part of civil society, NGOs have become involved in building and strengthening civil society while taking distance from the influence of the state and the market forces (Drabeck 1987; Banks and Hulme 2012).

During the last few decades, the notion of NGOs as part of civil society has been challenged. In the earlier days of NGOs, and particularly during the sixties and seventies, this notion appeared to make greater sense due to the grassroots orientation of NGOs. They were known to be closer to the people (Cernea 1988, 17–18; OECD 1988; Brown and Korten 1991), advocating for a transformative agenda (Bebbington et al. 2008) and building grassroots movements to respond to the needs of their communities. This dedication to community building and interaction is essentially what made them part of civil society in the early days of NGOs. As noted by David Lewis, Nazneen Kanji and Nuno S. Themudo (2021), the true strength of civil society is rooted in its environment and the opportunities that facilitate organized groups to foster interactions.

The decades of the eighties and nineties witnessed a massive proliferation of NGOs worldwide. While this proliferation of NGOs is discussed more later on in this chapter, let us only point out here that it was largely a direct consequence of the massive availability of funding sources for NGOs during that time. Kim Reimann (2006) convincingly reinforces this argument in his "top-down" approach to NGOs. He argues that the rapid growth of NGOs during the 1980s and 1990s resulted from national and international politics that opened new opportunities for funding for NGOs. He writes that "new international opportunities for funding and participation of NGOs have created a structural environment highly conducive to NGO growth" (46).

As funding increases, so does the number of NGOs and INGOs, yet their attachment to their fundamental cause decreases, bringing structural change (White 1999; Kaldor 2008; Townsend et al. 2004; Bebbington et al. 2008; Lewis and Kanji 2009; Elbers and Arts 2011; Lewis, Kanji and Themudo 2021). Many NGOs have begun to cater more to donors' needs to keep funding rather than focusing on the needs of the people they serve (Hudock 1999). Consequently, during the nineties, INGOs deployed throughout the developing world transformed the movement into service delivery under the umbrella of poverty reduction.

Concurrently, NGOs have become something close to the embodiment of civil society. This was well evidenced by the discourse of the global international aid system on developing, strengthening and building civil society through NGOs. International aid institutions such as the World Bank, USAID and UN agencies reinforced this discourse when channelling a substantial amount of their funding to civil society organizations, which largely refer to NGOs. With so much attention on strengthening civil society, NGOs have gained momentum and the powers of supra-organizations. Therefore, the claim that NGOs are part of civil society has become contested. In the last three decades, people have shifted their view of NGOs as being one segment of civil society to acting more like state-sponsored institutions. This shift in the evolution of NGOs is examined more closely later in the book.

Also, during the 1990s, neoliberalism reached its zenith as markets became increasingly globalized. It came to be understood that growth and development could occur only through engagement with the globalized economy. Open markets, trade liberalization and privatization of public goods and services transformed development into a private enterprise (McMichael 2008), which promised the betterment of people's conditions (Hintzen 2018). The post–World War II focus on national development to target improvement in conditions of national populations became overshadowed by this emphasis on participation in the globalized economy. This reality was particularly evident in the application of new policies by the United States and the International Financial Institutions (IFIs). As a result, development funding was diverted away from national governments and toward NGOs.

This massive availability of funding sources that propelled the proliferation of NGOs, as discussed earlier, is entangled with the neoliberalism policies of the 1980s and 1990s that favoured NGOs as new development strategies and a prime channel for poverty reduction assistance. Consequently, the 1990s saw a sevenfold increase in NGOs' official aid funding, from US$1 billion in 1970 to US$7 billion in 1990 (Ahmed and Potter 2006). As NGO funding began to increase significantly, so did their global presence. The number of NGOs grew significantly, rising from approximately six thousand in 1990 to an estimated sixty thousand by 1998 (Reagan 2003, 3). The shift in aid funding to NGOs increased their relevance and influence and simultaneously weakened the governments of developing countries (Dupuy 1997, 2005; Etienne 1997; Ferguson 2006; Schuller 2009, 2012).

Various scholars have focused on different aspects of the shift to NGOs. For instance, anthropologist Michel-Rolph Trouillot analysed the displacement of state functions and practices, mainly to supra-governmental organizations and NGOs. He framed this as indicative of the emergence of a "fragmented globality that questions the effectiveness of the national state as the primary site for economic exchange, political struggle, or cultural negotiation" (Trouillot 2001, 130). Similarly, James Ferguson pointed to the emergence of a "new sort of governance" in the wake of neoliberal policies that provoked a "rolling back" of the state. Consequently, he wrote, "at the same time, swarms of new nongovernmental organizations (NGOs), taking advantage of the shift in donor's policies that moved funding for projects away from mistrusted bureaucracies and into what was understood as more 'direct' or 'grassroots' channels of implementation" (Ferguson 2006, 38). Referring specifically to the case of Africa, Ferguson argued that "the new sort of governance" was supposed to be "both more democratic and more economically efficient" (Ferguson 2006, 38). However, this "rolling back of the state has provoked or exacerbated a far-reaching political crisis. As more and more of the functions of the state have been effectively 'outsourced' to NGOs, state capacity has deteriorated rapidly" (Ferguson 2006, 38). The state became nothing more than a "shadow state", which transforms the formal institutions of government into little more than empty shells (Ferguson 2006, 39).

The retreat of the national state was accompanied by a rise in poverty and scarcity across the Global South. During the 1990s, famine in Sudan and Somalia claimed the lives of millions. Across Ethiopia, Somalia and Kenya, droughts and hunger swept away vast populations and livelihoods. Faced with such disasters, populations in the global south relied increasingly more on NGOs for social services that once were provided by the state. In 2008, Roger C. Riddell wrote:

> The last 25 years have witnessed a phenomenal growth in the contribution of NGOs to the overall aid effort. NGOs run many times more development projects and programs than those funded by official aid agencies, and by 2004, the total value of NGO-funded activities was almost $24 billion, equivalent to over 30 per cent of overseas development

aid (ODA). In some countries, NGOs (including church-based agencies) are responsible for 10 per cent of health and education services – in a few countries, such as Haiti, probably in excess of 50 per cent. In Bangladesh, one NGO on its own, the Bangladesh Rural Advancement Committee (BRAC), provides basic curative and preventive health services to more than 97 million people, out of a total population of 143 million. (260)

Neoliberalism: When the "Un-usable" Becomes "Usable"

James Ferguson (2006) demonstrated that globalization has transformed Africa, which was particularly ignored by global capital. He notes that global capital now identifies a "usable" and an "unusable" Africa. The "usable Africa" refers to African territories with an abundance of natural resources, while the "unusable Africa" constitutes the rest of the continent and its poor people. Ferguson finds that global capital hops over the "unusable Africa" and lands on the "usable Africa".

This argument of "usable" and "unusable" areas, while quite solid, does not always encompass the reality of neoliberalism in the global South or even the reality of Africa. Aihwa Ong (2006) argues that neoliberalism operates as an exception. As such, neoliberalism can transform and mutate markets and populations in ways that benefit the capitalist economy. Ong demonstrates, for example, how a variety of neoliberal strategies have been developing and re-engineering political spaces and populations in the East and Southeast Asian states to benefit from market capitalism. Hence, even in the "unusable" parts of the world, neoliberalism can form engagements that allow the market to function and extract profits. This is made possible through forms of "exception", where global capital is granted exceptional authority and autonomy in areas of the country where people and resources are "excepted" from forms of state regulation. My argument is that neoliberalism creates conditions where non-usable populations are forced into global production and – to some extent – consumption.

Neoliberalism creates conditions where the state no longer caters to certain parts of the country and has instead abrogated its jurisdictional authority either to control by global capital or to depend on NGOs. In countries that heavily rely on NGOs, the NGOs tend to bridge the gap created by the withdrawal of the state (Schuller 2009). They assume the functions of the government in catering to the needs of the population. Concurrently, populations often come to rely on their economic initiatives. They do so by developing an informal economy or resorting to subsistence, accepting migration as segmented informal labour and even growing illegal drugs within their territories.

The goal of neoliberalism is to reduce state control of global economic processes and to create conditions for the insertion of its people and resources into these processes (Hintzen 2018; Ong 1999, 2006; Robinson 2014). Therefore, neoliberalism obliges usable labour to depend on the global economy and marginalizes non-usable labour because it does not have "effective demand". Once this occurs, the marginalized are constrained into the global economic circuits, which NGOs facilitate (Hintzen 2018). This process does not undermine the fact that local populations continue to revert to subsistence production as an alternative (Hintzen 2018). However, for the most part, non-usable labour and populations are forced into global production and, indirectly, global consumption. In the case of West Africa, for example, non-usable populations are forced into exploitable labour (mineral production of diamonds, coltan, etc.) in order to dramatically reduce production costs by forcing labourers to engage in their subsistence (Ferguson 2006). NGOs facilitate this process by providing food, healthcare and subsidized housing to those populations, which ensures the sustainability and reproduction of the system without the need for transfers from the state or capital.

My argument so far is that in the global capitalist market, nothing is wasted, but all is transformed; "unusable" populations are transformed into "usable" populations through the services provided by NGOs. Indeed, if we look at NGOs from a market-driven perspective, we will understand that they facilitate a massive transfer of goods, expenditures and technology to Third World populations. All equipment – the expensive SUVs, supplies, generators, etc. – that NGOs use to reach these remote areas, set up offices and conduct daily operations are primarily supplied by Northern countries. In this way, NGOs represent an important conduit between the global capitalist market and the Third World.

Because of NGOs, the "unusable" populations of the Third World have access to global consumer goods that otherwise would not be possible. One may argue that the transfer of goods and technology to the Third World is not the primary function of NGOs. They only indirectly serve this purpose, a fact that I do not overlook in this study.

In the age of globalization, flexibility remains one of the main characteristics of market capitalism. In *The Condition of Postmodernity* (1989), David Harvey identifies late capitalism as a "regime of flexible accumulation". In terms of capital, flexibility refers to the ability to move capital both in terms of production location and financial assets, as well as the production of different goods and services. In terms of labour, flexibility refers to the ability to migrate and do different types of jobs. In short, capital moves around the world, as do people. We have witnessed that more people are travelling internationally for better jobs and greater access to economic gains. Ong (1999) particularly places this flexibility in the cultural logic of the global capitalism system. As she puts it:

> In their quest to accumulate capital and social prestige in the global arena, subjects emphasize, and are regulated by, practices favoring flexibility, mobility, and repositioning in relation to the markets, governments, and cultural regimes. These logic and practices are produced within particular structures of meaning about family, gender, nationality, class mobility, and social power. (6)

The practice of "flexibility, mobility, and repositioning" (Ong 1999, 6) is on the rise in the Third World due to the presence of NGOs. In the countries where northern NGOs operate on a large scale, such as Haiti and Kenya, one can notice not only a movement of capital, goods and technology but also of people and technocrats. These people move because, even as NGO workers, they are central actors in the global economy. Indeed, most of the NGOs' directors and high-ranking personnel come from Western countries. Thus, they are critical to the maintenance of global capitalism by reducing the need for the transfer of revenues from profit into welfare, hence contributing to super profits and low taxes. In the case of Haiti, particularly after the 2010 earthquake, NGO presence – in addition to other bilateral and multilateral agencies – has led to an escalation in the number of expatriates in the country (Hintzen 2019; United States Department of Commerce 2019) who saw in post-earthquake rehabilitation an opportunity not only for economic gain but also for prestige and power.

My research on NGOs in Haiti following the 2010 earthquake began with an observation of the transnational flow of people and money. Later, my focus shifted to investigating both the effectiveness and limitations of NGOs in delivering disaster relief in a way that can produce sustainable development outcomes based on the study of Haiti. NGOs are critical to neoliberal transnational capital. They also contribute to economic leakage and limit backward and forward linkages since their wages are either earned in or returned to their home countries or used for foreign breakdown.

Some Key Conceptual Terms

In the context of this book, some conceptual terms will be frequently employed. While these terms appear very familiar, their precise meanings within the context of the analysis presented in this book merit explicit clarification. There is nothing too complex about the nuances of those conceptual terms. Still, it is nevertheless important to clarify them in this chapter to ensure that the reader grasps their specific meanings and distinctions as intended within the context of the argument made in this book.

Hazards

In the context of this book, *hazards* refer to events arising from natural forces. Particularly, I refer to physical events such as earthquakes, tornadoes, volcanic eruptions, hurricanes, landslides, floods and similar forms of natural events. Hazards exist independently of our ability to prevent them from happening. They come with the potential for harm and cause damage to life, property, health and the economy, as well as disturb the order of things. However, despite our inability to prevent their occurrences, remarkable progress has been made in relation to early predictions and the identification of early warning signs. Remarkable progress has also been made in developing mitigation strategies and adaptation to natural hazards. Therefore, their potential to bring calamities often depends on human actions and inactions. When natural hazards trigger severe damage to life and property and disrupt the normal functioning of a society, they are referred to in this book as natural disasters.

Natural Disasters

This book is concerned primarily with natural disasters. Yet, disasters can be triggered by events and processes other than natural. A technological failure may trigger massive devastation, immense losses and unfortunate severe health consequences. However, when talking about disasters or natural disasters, this book references major adverse physical events that are caused by natural hazards. Natural hazards, even the most intense ones, do not automatically transform into disasters. Disasters occur when the disruptions caused by a natural hazard exceed the capacity of the affected community to cope using the resources they have at their disposal (ISDR 2004; Prasad and Francescutti 2017).

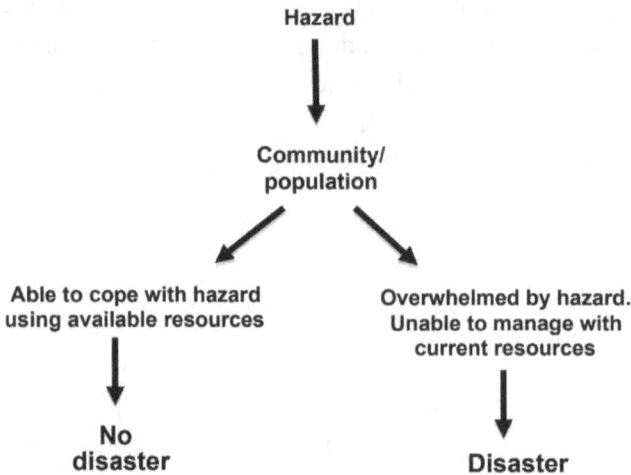

Hazard

↓

Community/ population

↙   ↘

Able to cope with hazard using available resources

Overwhelmed by hazard. Unable to manage with current resources

↓   ↓

No disaster

Disaster

Figure 1.1:   Differentiating between a Hazard and a Disaster
Source: Prasad and Francescutti 2017, 215

To illustrate, the state of California regularly experiences earthquakes; however, they cause very little to no disruption at all. The 7.1 magnitude earthquake[3] that struck the city of Ridgecrest in California caused relatively minor damage and no deaths (Los Angeles Times 2019). An event is classified as a disaster based on the criteria established by the Center for Research on Epidemiology of Disasters (CRED). According to CRED, an event is a disaster if any of the following criteria is met after the event (Guha-Sapir et al. 2012):

- Ten or more people were reported killed;
- One hundred or more people reported being affected;
- Declaration of state of emergency;
- Call for international assistance.

Natural disasters, in this context, underline the complex interactions between the environment and human structures. Human structures can mitigate the impacts of natural hazards. However, they can also create conditions for even a regular natural event, such as torrential rain, to become a destructive natural disaster. When this situation occurs, I call it a human-made disaster.

Human-made Disaster

Natural disasters are often caused by nature or the environment, but also often have a human origin. However, when talking about human-made disasters, the literature especially signals the types of disasters that are the result of human mistakes. Those human mistakes include but are not limited to, large-scale fires, chemical spills, nuclear accidents, and structural collapses and failures. Wars and terrorist attacks, to some extent, can also be considered as human-made disasters. My perspective of human-made disasters does not only include technological and chemical accidents; it encompasses natural disasters that are the result of social and economic processes that create risks and transform natural events into pervasive natural disasters.

Risks

This book adopts the United Nations' definition of risks as "the probability of harmful consequences, or expected losses (deaths, injuries, property, livelihoods, economic activity disrupted or environment damaged) resulting from interactions between natural or human-induced hazards and vulnerable conditions" (ISDR 2004). The nature and causes of risk may nevertheless vary according to the forms of societies. Developed societies face risks that correlate with their level of wealth, their technological advances and the insecurities that emanate from the modernization of life itself. For example, in more developed countries, there is a great level of anxiety about artificial intelligence, nuclear accidents or viruses that can emerge from human activities. In developing countries, on the other hand, risks are associated with environmental issues and vulnerabilities embedded in poor living conditions. Conventionally, risks are understood through a sample formula: Risks = Hazards x Vulnerabilities. In some fields, exposure is additionally considered, particularly focusing on the physical aspects of vulnerability. In that way, Risks = Hazards x Vulnerabilities + Exposure.

Methods and Expected Impacts

This book emerges from my doctoral research, which focused on whether disaster resilience was built into the post-quake NGO-provided relief in Haiti. The study was conducted in Port-au-Prince. Port-au-Prince is divided into eight communes,[4] but the study focused on three communes that were the most affected by the earthquake: Carrefour, the commune of Port-au-Prince (which is the city downtown) and Delmas. A commune represents the third-level administrative division in Haiti. The country is organized around four levels of administrative divisions: *Department, Arrondissements, Communes* and *Communal Sections*: The country is divided into 10 departments. The departments are subdivided in 42 arrondissements, 144 communes and 571 Communal Sections (Haiti Libre 2015; Olivier 2015).

The data for this research were gathered through institutional ethnography, document analysis, semi-structured interviews and a household survey. I collected the data in three phases over ten months, from August 2018 to May 2019. The methodology is detailed in the appendix.

The book analyses the role of NGOs in disaster relief and management and the possibility of their involvement in producing sustainable development outcomes. It is helpful for this research to situate my theoretical understanding of the concept of development, map how relief could build resilient communities as part of development goals and assess the role of NGOs in this process. The book comes with the prospect of breaking new ground by linking long-term development goals with building resilience to disasters.

This book advances several fields of inquiry, including the sociology of development, disaster and resilience studies, the study of NGOs, disaster management and preparedness and political economy. It contributes to rapidly expanding literature that links disaster relief and development. In its engagement with the fraught issue of development and resilience, the study also contributes to a new practical paradigm; it articulates a locally centred strategy combined with the assistance of NGOs and showcases the potential efficacy of this combination to realize developmental goals. The book promotes the idea of building resilient communities as the primary goal of development projects in disaster-prone areas. Analysis from the book also extends to NGOs' day-to-day operations in the wake of disaster, viewing such organizations as engines of development as opposed to perennial relief management organizations.

This book will also make significant contributions to understanding the ways in which NGOs can successfully deliver and implement disaster aid in the context of a weakened state. Building on the lessons learned from past interventions of NGOs, this research investigates both the limits and possibilities of NGO-provided aid. It also frames what successful delivery of disaster aid entails and thus focuses on gaining a better understanding of the relationship between disaster aid and development. Drawing on the argument that disasters occur because of a lack of development, this book argues that the successful delivery of disaster aid must be development-oriented. This requires reducing vulnerabilities, increasing capacities and building resilient communities. Finally, the book is based on transformative research that can have immediate and significant policy implications as related to NGOs in Haiti, the way aid has been delivered and implemented and the pursuit of ongoing development goals. The book will allow the international community to make better investments in disaster relief and aid in developing countries and to save funds in the future by pursuing building disaster-resilient communities as a fundamental development goal.

The Structure of the Book

The book is divided into seven chapters. In chapter 2, I briefly theorize the issue of climate change and the rise of natural disasters since the 1960s. Then, I address the changing relationship between disaster aid and development. To illustrate this changing relationship, I analyse the historical evolution of disaster as a concept since the 1950s. I demonstrate how a change of thinking in disaster studies during the 1980s and 1990s has brought the concept of development into the disaster discourse. I also critically examine disaster aid. I unpack the humanitarian, moral, political and economic arguments that underpin disaster aid. I conclude the chapter with the Hyogo Conference on Disaster Reduction's call for disaster aid to be delivered and implemented in ways that can promote development and reduce vulnerability to future disasters. The remainder of the chapter focuses particularly on development. I survey three developmental approaches. I analyse Amartya Sen's approach, which equates development to freedom. I examine Hintzen's approach, which is both a continuity and a critique of Sen's approach. While Hintzen shares the idea of development as freedom, he poses the systematic conditions for that freedom to flourish, which is possible only under the conditions of democracy and good governance. I also examine M. Anderson and P. Woodrow's approach, which views development as the process by which capacities are increased and vulnerabilities decreased.

Chapter 3 critically examines the political and economic factors that led to Haiti's reliance on NGOs. This chapter is fundamental to my thesis, as it investigates how neoliberalism destroyed the Haitian economy and created a heavy reliance on NGOs. I argue in this chapter that neoliberalism has been implemented in Haiti in two phases: The first phase corresponds to the beginning of the implementation during the 1980s; the second articulates a full implementation of neoliberal policies in Haiti.

Chapter 4 analyses the political, economic and demographic conditions of the country before the 2010 earthquake. I use Trouillot's framework of the "state against the nation" to make sense of the case of Haiti. Trouillot has demonstrated that, under the Duvalier regime, the state was used as an instrument against the nation. While Trouillot's framework was initially applied in the context of Duvalier's regime, I argue in this chapter that in the post-Duvalier era, the state continues to be used as a weapon against the nation.

Chapter 5 focuses on relief intervention efforts in the wake of the 2010 earthquake. I emphasize the language used in an International Donors' Conference around terms such as "build back better", "recovery and rebuilding" and "new Haiti". I explore the disjunctures between the language used and what was put into practice. In this chapter, I also present and analyse the results of the survey conducted to determine the perceived effectiveness of NGO intervention. I measure this against objectives presented at an International Donors' Conference held in New York and the action plan developed under the direction of the Haitian government.

Chapter 6 examines the failure of post-disaster intervention to address existing vulnerabilities and realize development transformation. As evidence of this failure, I highlight the fact that even the major government buildings have yet to be rebuilt ten years after the earthquake. I also demonstrate that this failure exacerbated existing vulnerabilities and created new ones. As an alternative, I argue for effective collaboration with NGOs, local governments and organizations.

In chapter 7, I argue for linking relief, rehabilitation and reconstruction. I demonstrate that rehabilitation and reconstruction need to coexist for a post-disaster intervention to realize development transformation and produce resilience to disaster. I conclude the chapter on a positive note by highlighting two NGO projects that demonstrate good practices for building resilient communities.

TWO

Disaster Aid, NGOs and Development in the Age of Climate Change

Today we are faced with a challenge that calls for a shift in our thinking, so that humanity stops threatening its life-support system.

Wangari Maathai
Nobel Peace Prize Winner, 2004.

This book is located at the intersection of three broad bodies of scholarly focus: disaster aid/relief, NGOs and development. Before critically analysing these three approaches, it is important to note that the literature on disaster research has – until the end of the twentieth century – been fragmented along disciplinary and analytical frameworks. While sociologists tended to focus on organizational behaviour during disasters, geographers posited the problem of place, and political scientists addressed risk assessment policies and practices (Oliver-Smith 2001). However, this study draws on the political economy perspective that has dominated the discourse on disasters since the 1980s. By specifically analysing natural disasters in the Third World, this perspective identifies the root causes of disasters as they relate more to social and economic conditions than to natural phenomena (Blaikie 1994; Blaikie et al. 1994; Cannon 1994; Hewitt 1983, 1997; Hilhorst 2004; Hilhorst and Bankoff 2004; Lavell 1994; Oliver-Smith 2004). From this perspective, disasters are understood as a product of social processes that create unequal exposure to hazards and risks, leaving some people more vulnerable to disasters than others (Hilhorst and Bankoff 2004). Poverty, social exclusion, chronic malnutrition and lack of effective development constitute some of the primary roots of disasters (Blaikie et al. 1994; Hewitt 1997). The fact that those conditions are more present in developing countries explains the frequency of disasters in such areas (Hilhorst 2004; Ward and Shively 2017).

Building on that premise, the main argument of my research is that to foster disaster resilience in developing countries, disaster relief must centre development in its interventions to minimize future vulnerability and be delivered in a manner that advances this goal.

Disaster Aid: Context and Evolution

The concept of "disaster" refers to a "serious disruption of the functioning of a community or a society causing widespread human, material, economic or environmental losses which exceed the ability of the affected community or society to cope using its own resources" (UN 2004, 17). In the wake of a disaster, we often witness an outpouring of assistance given to the affected populations. This assistance is generally referred to as "humanitarian aid", "emergency relief", "disaster aid" or simply "relief". The agencies providing aid are commonly known as "humanitarian agencies". Among these, the United Nations agencies and NGOs are the largest and most visible (Riddell 2008). Thus, grappling with how best to deliver disaster relief requires first that we address the problem of disasters.

Living Dangerously: Climate Change and the Rise of Natural Disasters

We are living in a time of deep uncertainty, largely due to climate change. Climate change, particularly as it causes rising temperatures and changing rainfall patterns, will continue to affect human livelihood and increase both the frequency and magnitude of weather-related hazards (Schipper and Pelling 2006). The United Nations Intergovernmental Panel on Climate Change (IPCC) reports that since the late nineteenth century, the average global surface temperature has increased by 0.6 degrees centigrade. It is projected that the average surface air temperature will increase between 1.4 and 4.4 degrees centigrade by 2100 (IPCC 2023). It is also projected that average global sea levels will rise between 0.09 metres and 0.88 metres by 2100 (Dore and Etkin 2003). While it is difficult to foresee what impacts these changes will have, climate change certainly represents a threat to the environment and humanity, as evidenced by the increasing frequency of natural disasters. We are, therefore, living dangerously (Reid 2014). Whether in the United States, China, Europe or the Caribbean, increasing numbers of lives are lost every year as a result of catastrophic climate extremes.

However, it is widely recognized that climate change's impacts have caused dramatically disparate levels of destruction in different places. The Johannesburg Declaration on Sustainable Development notes that "the adverse effects of climate change are already evident, natural disasters are more frequent and more devastating, and developing countries more vulnerable". Whether analysing disaster frequency in developed or developing countries, it is important to situate the debate within the context of economic development.

The Changing Relationship between Disaster and Development

Academically and practically, the relationship between disaster and development has been shifting over the recent decades. In this section, I will illustrate how the two have been linked, especially since the 1960s.

The Dark Decades (1960s–70s)

At the end of the nineteenth century, the world was already divided into poor countries and rich countries. The post–World War II period rendered this geographical divide clearer as poverty became increasingly less apparent. The decolonization of African countries at the end of the 1950s and during the 1960s unveiled a hidden form of human suffering that was largely unknown to the world until then. Famine and abject poverty were "discovered". A sizable population in the world was deemed traditional, backward and underdeveloped. Against the backdrop of this reality, the discourse of development took root. Modernization, viewed as economic development, was presented as the necessary force capable of driving traditional societies from backwardness (Escobar 1997). This approach was crystallized in Walt Rostow's book *The Stages of Economic Growth* published in 1960, in which Rostow prescribed the stages through which undeveloped societies must pass to become developed. Development since then has been associated with progress and economic growth. It is displayed through infrastructure building, planned urbanization, availability of public services and a systematic reduction of poverty.

When it comes to the scholarly relationship between disaster and development, I call the 1960s and 1970s the dark decades. It was a period when no valuable work to link disaster and development was attempted. Disasters were seen as neither related to nor exacerbated by underdevelopment. Instead, disasters were attributed to the environment and nature (Bolt 1978). They were viewed as a consequence of "extremes in geophysical processes" (Hewitt 1983, 4). Because disasters were attributed to the environment and nature, they were treated as something outside of society (Hewitt 1983). In this regard, Hewitt writes:

> The geography of disaster is an archipelago of isolated misfortunes. Each is seen as localized disorganization of space, projected upon the extensive map of human geography in a more or less random way due to independent events in the geographical realms of atmosphere, hydrosphere, and lithosphere. More specifically, each disaster is an unplanned hole or rupture in the fabric of productive and orderly human relations with habitat or 'natural resources'. (Hewitt 1945, 13)

In this environmentally deterministic view, terms such as "misfortune", "act of God" (Fisher 1998), "unusual events" (Toblin 1977) and "accidents" (Haddon, Suchman and Klein 1964) were used to explain disasters. By describing disaster in this way, the environmental determinists created a discourse that reduced disasters to unmanaged, unexpected and unprecedented phenomena. This discourse did not allow for the possibility that humans might pre-emptively mitigate the impact of disasters. The approach of environmental determinism led researchers, naturally, to focus on appropriate reactions to disasters and effective emergency measures after the disaster had occurred.

Consequently, researchers and scholars failed to focus on factors that produced disasters but instead on disaster response.

Emergence of Disaster Behaviour and Crisis Management

Very few empirical studies were conducted on disasters in the early twentieth century. Samuel Prince conducted the first systematic study of disaster in 1920 in his doctoral dissertation on the Halifax explosion. Prince's dissertation focused on the organizational response to the explosion when the French cargo ship *Mont Blanc,* which carried explosives, collided with a Norwegian vessel on the morning of December 1917 (Fisher 1984; Perry 2006). The explosion, the largest human-induced recorded at that time, killed at least 1,782 people in Halifax, located in the Canadian province of Nova Scotia (Knauer 2012; Ruffman et al. 1994). Lowell Julliard Carr (1932) made a significant contribution to the nascent field when in 1932 he published his paper entitled "Disaster and the Sequence-Pattern Concept of Social Change". Through his work, Carr pioneered the social science approach to disasters that ascribes the root of disasters to social change.

Nevertheless, it was at the beginning of the second half of the century that growing interest in disaster studies began to spark. Interests particularly emerged from the field of geography under the umbrella of natural hazard studies with a focus on building and land development (Bavel et al. 2020). Guilbert F. White, geographer and the early pioneer of Hazard research, was very influential in the development of the field. His ground-breaking work *Human Adjustment to Floods,* published in 1945, convincingly argued, "floods are an act of God, but losses from floods are largely an act of man". In 1976, Gilbert White created the Natural Hazards Research and Information Center, known today as the Natural Hazards Center, at the University of Colorado. His work, the assessment of the status of natural hazards research in the United States, was funded by the Natural Science Foundation. Throughout the second half of the century, White continued to conduct research on floodplain management in the United States and developing countries.

Almost at the same time, specifically in the 1960s, social scientists began to turn their attention to the socio-economic and behavioural impacts of disasters. They formulated what came to be known as the behavioural school. They began to look at how people and institutions respond to disasters. A key figure of this period was Enrico H. Quarantelli, the founder of the Disaster Research Center, the first social research centre on disaster in the United States (Fisher 1998; Quarantelli 2002). Other important scholars, such as Thomas E. Drabek, Russell R. Dynes and Charles Fritz, were also part of the behavioural school on disasters. These scholars explored disaster as a social problem. Their focus was on the behaviour of individuals and organizations toward mitigating damage and their responses to actual disasters and potential threats posed by their occurrence.

The challenge for this period was to bring a clear definition that embraces the social dimension of disasters. With the publication of his paper in 1932, Carr had already established the groundwork for a basic social definition of disaster that future disaster scholars will stand on to develop more comprehensive definitions of disasters. Carr (1932), indeed, viewed disasters as the "collapse of the cultural protections" (211). For Carr, if the protections work, the dam retains the water and the walls sustain the earthquake, there is no disaster (Perry 2006). Other scholars proposed definitions that I am not considering here. However, a definition worth noting here came from Charles Fritz (1961). Fritz characterized disaster as

> actual and threatened accidental or uncontrollable events that are concentrated in time and space, in which a society, or a relatively self-sufficient subdivision of a society undergoes severe danger and incurs such losses to its members and physical appurtenances that the social structure is disrupted and the fulfillment of all or some of the essential functions of the society, or its subdivision, is prevented.

Other impactful contributions in defining disasters were made by Quarantelli and Dynes, who co-founded the Disaster Research Center in 1963 and contributed to the training of numerous disaster researchers. Particularly, Quarantelli's work looks at disasters through a variety of defining characteristics. According to Quarantelli, disasters 1) are sudden-onset occasions, 2) seriously disrupt the routines of collective units, 3) cause the adoption of unplanned courses of action to adjust to disruption, 4) have unexpected life histories designated in social space in time and 5) pose a danger to valued social objects (Perry 2006, 10).

Sociologists brought new insights to disaster studies during the 1970s. Nevertheless, Kenneth Hewitt, a political geographer, found that the sociological approach reinforced what he called the "geophysicalist dominant view" of disasters (Hewitt 1983). Hewitt criticized the sociologists' argument that indicated that a greater number of people are vulnerable to natural disasters, mainly because they are located in dangerous areas (Oliver-Smith and Hoffman 2001). Hewitt critiqued disaster sociologists such as Enrico Quarantelli and Russell Dynes for emphasizing human behaviours to address pre-existing conditions such as overpopulation, risk areas and accidental features of places and societies. Hewitt called those efforts "window dressing, dealing with issues that do not penetrate beyond conceptual preambles" (Hewitt 1983, 16). He argued that the dominant view placed disaster outside the structural order and contemporary social developments that pervade everyday life and cause disasters in the first place (Hewitt 1983, 25). Hewitt called for a break with the past.

Paradigm Shift in Disaster Studies (1980s–90s)

The publication of *Interpretations of Calamity* in 1983, edited by Kenneth Hewitt, resulted in a shift in the approach to disasters. In a critique of the then-dominant perspective on disasters, which he believed was insensitive to human development and social inequalities, Hewitt stated in the introduction to the volume:

> The dominant view then belongs to a historically special culture that seeks to interpret the world through its underpinnings in material phenomena and mechanism. Disaster remains a difficult, perhaps a decisive, test of such explanations. It is a deliberate problem for prevailing interpretations of nature and human development and the way they are appropriated by technical institutions. Disaster, taken literally, however, suggests revolutionary change. (18)

Thus, Hewitt called for a fundamental change – what scholars such as Thomas Kuhn (1962) called a "paradigm shift" – in the way we thought about and understood disasters. Of the factors that contributed to

Hewitt's decision to call for a shift in disaster research, we can consider two in particular:

1. Since the 1960s, there has been a considerable increase in natural disasters (Janse and Flier 2014; Grove 2010; Pelling 2003). This increase proportionally affects developing countries, which underscores a relationship between disaster and underdevelopment. Indeed, Mark Pelling (2002, 2003) accounts for the fact that the number of natural disasters reported per annum has doubled since the 1960s. During the 1980s and 1990s, scholars have observed a disproportionate occurrence of disasters in developing countries. For example, it was observed that during the 1990s, 96 per cent of the annual average number of persons killed and 99 per cent of people affected by hazards resided outside the United States, Canada and Europe (Walker and Walter 2000, 173–75). This disproportionate occurrence underlines the argument that disasters were not merely a consequence of geographic position but instead of demographic and economic differences, thus highlighting that inhabitants of developing countries are more likely to die from disasters (Bankoff 2004).

2. We must also consider the uneven impacts of disasters: As disasters increase in the developing world, the most vulnerable are the most affected. Following the 1976 earthquake in Guatemala, Marxist disaster scholars began to take a closer look at the relationship between social and economic conditions as related to disasters, as it was evident that low-income and indigenous people were struck harder by the earthquake (Blaikie 1994; Wisner 2003). More disaster scholars began to study disaster through a political-economic lens. It became clear that social power and material conditions had a profound effect on the social distribution of risk (Blaikie 1994; Wisner 1993a, 1996, 1998). Indeed, numerous disasters occurred mostly as a result of inequality, population displacement and other material conditions that particularly affected the poor.

Ben Wisner cites many examples that support this argument. Among them is the case of Hurricane Mitchell, which killed thirty thousand people in Honduras and Nicaragua in 1998 (Wisner 2003). He argues that the impact of the hurricane is a consequence of the displacement of the population by agri-businesses, which forced them to live in unsafe conditions.

Considering the structural factors that shape the social and economic distribution of risk, Terry Cannon made a critical distinction between hazards and disasters. He argued that while hazards are natural phenomena, disasters are not. Instead, disasters are symptomatic of social processes that generate unequal exposure to risk, which makes some people more vulnerable than others (Cannon 1994, 14–19). By analysing disasters through the lens of vulnerability, we can also gain insight into the relationship between disaster and development. The African NGO Periperi defines vulnerability as a "set of prevailing or consequential conditions composed of physical, socio-economic, and/ or political factors that adversely affect the ability to respond to events" (Holloway, quoted in Delica-Willison and Willison 2003, 148). Those factors impact the social and economic conditions in underdeveloped communities. Blaikie et al. (1994) strengthened this argument by pointing out that "vulnerability is deeply rooted, and fundamental solutions involve political change, radical reform of the international economic system, and the development of public policy to protect rather than exploit people and nature" (233).

Disaster, Climate Change and Development: A Global Concern

The twenty-first century began with increased global concerns about climate change as the number of disasters and related economic losses continue to increase. For example, between 1990 and 1999, there were a total of eighty-two major disasters. The resulting economic losses totalled US$535 billion (UN 2004, 45). This shows that climate-related natural hazards have the potential to hinder or even reverse years of development gains and make development goals even more difficult to achieve in underdeveloped areas (Dilley et al. 2005; Grove 2010; Schipper and Pelling 2006). Considering the scope of danger that

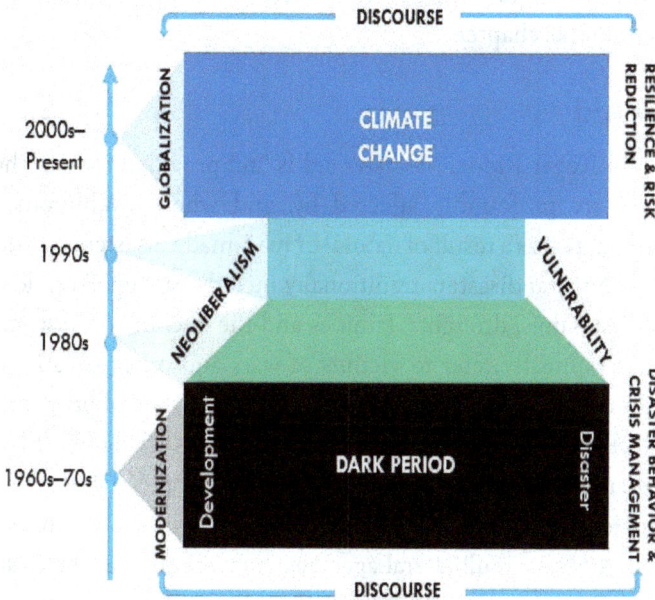

Figure 2.1: The Historical Relationship between Disaster and Development
Source: Figure Designed by Author

climate change may represent to development, the UN has adopted several resolutions intended to address the connection between disaster and development.

One example is The UN Millennium Development Goals, adopted in 2000, which recommended that national governments incorporate disaster risk reductions into national development policies. The 2005 Hyogo Framework for Action argued that a priority for action should be to use "knowledge, innovation, and education to build a culture of safety and resilience at all levels". The 2015 Sendai for Disaster Risk Reduction also placed resilience at the centre of disaster risk reduction. These are based on the idea that resilience is "the capacity of a system, community or society potentially exposed to hazards to adapt, by resisting or changing in order to reach and maintain an acceptable level of functioning and structure" (UN 2004, 16). In this book, I argue that an effective delivery of disaster aid must consider a development strategy that fosters a culture of resilience as a necessary condition, which I will discuss later in this chapter.

Disaster Aid

According to Roger Riddell, disaster aid is "aid provided to help those whose lives are profoundly affected by, and whose livelihoods are immediately at risk as a result of natural or man-made disasters" (Riddell 2008, 311). Natural disasters traditionally include earthquakes, floods, hurricanes, tsunamis, droughts, famines and the like. In contrast, man-made disasters mostly refer to victims of wars and other situations of severe political, economic and social breakdowns. The aid provided to people affected by disasters (natural or man-made) is often referred to as humanitarian aid or assistance, relief or emergency relief. Disaster aid is largely provided by four main agencies: government official donors such as the United States, multilateral agencies, humanitarian agencies such as United Nations agencies and NGOs. The purpose of humanitarian aid is to save lives, alleviate suffering and enable people who are suffering to maintain their dignity during and after a disaster (OECD 2004a).

The literature on disaster aid has paid a great deal of attention to natural disasters due to the fact that natural disasters have increased since the 1960s, as explained earlier (O'Byrne 2013; Riddell 2008; Schipper and Pelling 2006). Riddell stresses that "the total number of [annual] disasters reported since the mid-1950s rose from fewer than 80 in the mid-1960s to more than 200 by the end of the 1970s. This number rose further to 300 by the start of the 1990s, to over 700 by the turn of the century, and to almost 850 by 2005" (Riddell 2008, 314). Just as the number of disasters has risen, the damage and loss of human lives resulting from such disasters are also skyrocketing.

It has been demonstrated that damages are often unevenly distributed, specifically the loss of human lives. Disaster mortality is far greater in poor countries. Darren O'Byrne (2013), in his article "Dealing with Disasters in an Age of Globalized Sentiment: Testing the Boundaries of the Cosmopolitan Ideal?" offers an informative list of natural disasters that have occurred in recent years, along with the damage they have caused. This list includes Hurricane Katrina, which took the lives of

1,836 people in 2005 in the United States. In China, sixty-nine thousand people were killed as a result of an earthquake in 2009, and one hundred and forty-six thousand people lost their lives in Burma during the same year. Wildfires killed about fifty-six thousand people in Russia in 2010, preceded by another 173 wildfire-related deaths in 2009. In Haiti, the massive earthquake in January 2010 took the lives of approximately two hundred and thirty thousand and severely destroyed the capital city of Port-au-Prince. On 27 February 2010, an earthquake killed around five hundred people in Chile and many more were injured. In Afghanistan, 172 people were killed in February of the same year as a result of thirty-six avalanches. The following year, an earthquake that ravaged part of New Zealand killed 181 people. In addition to this list, we can add that more recently, in 2017, Hurricane Maria devastated the northeastern Caribbean, causing 3,059 deaths. In 2019, the powerful category 5 Hurricane Dorian severely struck the Bahamas, killed approximately 245 people and left more than 70,000 people homeless.

This list is far from exhaustive, but it nevertheless demonstrates the consistency of disasters, their potential for immense destruction, and where human casualties often occur. Furthermore, the United Nations Development Program (UNDP 2004) reports that only 11 per cent of the people exposed to droughts, windstorms, floods and earthquakes live in low-income countries. Yet, those countries mentioned above represent 53 per cent of people who lost their lives as a result of those types of natural disasters. The World Bank (2004) also notes that when taking account of damages in terms of gross domestic product (GDP), poor countries' economic losses far exceed those of rich countries. As the number of disasters and level of damages rise, the international community has responded to correspondingly increasing appeals for disaster aid. Complete data is not available to assess the degree to which the international community has responded to disasters in developing countries. However, it is estimated that in 2004, the total humanitarian aid globally amounted to US$12.4 billion. When private donations are included, the amount is estimated to have reached US$15 billion (Riddell 2008). J.V. Henderson and Y.S. Lee (2015) reported that Indonesia alone received US$7.7 billion over a four-year period in the wake of the 2004 tsunami. This leads us to ask: What is the logic behind funnelling so much money to disaster aid?

There is a problem in the rationale behind the allocation of disaster aid. A moral argument is often evoked to justify humanitarian assistance (Degnbol-Martinussen and Engberg-Pedersen 2003). Based on this moral argument, a well-off person must help those who are suffering and have poor access to resources. O'Byrne (2013) locates his moral argument within the framework of the "cosmopolitan ideal". This is derived from the capitalist ethic and linked to a form of cultural capital that makes the citizens of the West reflect on their global responsibility. It is made possible by the global media, which has transformed tragedies into global events (O'Byrne 2013). However, this moral argument fails to recognize that most humanitarian aid is institutional (bilateral, multilateral and NGO-based – even though the latter may depend on private personal contributions). In addition, it is believed that individual responsibility cannot solve problems that demand institutional responses.

Disaster aid is the result of a much more complex reality. Degnbol-Martinussen and Engberg-Pedersen (2003) show that donors are often motivated by self-interest, as they argue that assistance to poor countries will benefit rich countries in the long term. Aid, then, is built into the structural order that produces underdevelopment in the first place and contributes to the factors that cause disasters because it feeds donors' interests. My argument so far is that the way aid is given and allocated prevents its efficacy. Therefore, disaster aid needs to be allocated in new ways that can address the structural realities that produce disasters.

In addition to addressing structural problems that produce disasters, humanitarian aid needs to be given impartially and respectfully. Riddell, in his book *Does Foreign Aid Really Help?* (Riddell 2008, 312), stresses four principles that must guide the allocation of humanitarian aid and that underscore the idea of respect and impartiality:

1. The principle of impartiality: According to this principle, humanitarian aid should be provided solely on the basis of need and without discrimination based on race, religion, gender, age, nationality, ethnicity or political affiliation.

2. The principle of neutrality: Assistance is provided to all civilians in need and does not favour one side or the other in a conflict or war.

3. The principle of independence: It is broadly accepted that aid should be provided independently to ensure its neutrality.

4. The principle of unconditionality: It is universally acknowledged that aid given based on need requires no repayment from the population receiving such assistance.

Such an argument about allocating aid in ways that can address social and economic causes of disaster is not necessarily new. Particularly, the 2005 Hyogo Conference on Disaster Risk Reduction called for disaster aid to be delivered and implemented in ways that could promote development, reduce vulnerability and increase resilience to future disasters. This begs the question as to what form of development can produce resilience. If development policy produces disaster and prevents resilience, then how can these policies be reformulated? Before addressing those questions, let us briefly discuss NGOs.

NGOs, Classification and Potential Contribution to Development

NGOs are "private organizations that pursue activities to relieve suffering, promote the interest of the poor, protect the environment, provide basic social services, or undertake community development" (World Bank 1995, 7). Scholars have attempted to classify them into several categories according to their work. In this chapter, I use the work of Shamima Ahmed and David Potter (2006), who categorize NGOs according to their role in international politics. These two scholars group them according to the following roles: political, advocacy and lobbying, agenda setting, relief and social and economic development (37).

Political Roles

Many NGOs aim to challenge the political, social and economic structures that breed poverty and inequality. Although NGOs are generally known as non-political organizations, Ahmed and Potter

(2006) report that many NGOs, both Northern and Southern, have begun to define themselves by their political, rather than economic, objectives as they engage in advocacy, lobbying and agenda-setting activities.

Advocacy and Lobbying

The NGOs that engage in advocacy and lobbying are, according to Margaret Keck and Kathryn Sikkink, those that "plead the cause of others or defend a cause or proposition. Advocacy captures what is unique about these transnational networks: they are organized to promote causes, principled ideas, and norms, and they often involve individuals advocating policy changes that can easily link to a rationalist understanding of their interests" (1998, 9).

Agenda-setting

This category describes NGOs that address specific social issues, such as women's equality, environmentalism or indigenous rights, and put these issues on the political agenda. Many social ills have been addressed because of the work of NGOs. For example, women's rights and environmental protection have been on political agendas primarily because of the work of NGOs. Greenpeace and Consumer International are both examples of agenda-setting organizations.

Relief

According to Ahmed and Potter (2006), NGOs' role for most of the twentieth century was that of charity and relief. This trend started with Christian missionary organizations that strove to address both spiritual and material poverty. John Degnbol-Marinussen and Poul Engberg-Pedersen (2005), in tracing the origin of NGOs, argue that most NGOs grew out of relief activities. For example, the Red Cross, Red Crescent, Médecins sans Frontières (Doctors without Borders) and Oxfam were all born out of relief efforts. Oxfam, one of the most widely known NGOs, was initially created to provide relief to Greece during wartime. Many of these organizations later became development-oriented.

Social and Economic Development

The involvement of NGOs in development has emerged from the reality that relief and charity work address short-term needs rather than long-term development problems (Ahmed and Potter 2006; Anderson and Woodrow 1989; Degnbol-Marinussen and Engberg-Pedersen 2005; Pelling 2004; Sirleaf 1993). Another essential element that explains this involvement is the mandate of the United States Congress to use American bilateral aid in a way that focuses more on the needs of the very poor in developing countries. In 1973, the United States Congress declared that foreign aid was to "be carried out to the maximum extent possible through the private sector, particularly those institutions which already have ties in the developing areas, such as educational institutions, cooperatives, credit unions, and voluntary agencies" (Ahmed and Potter 2006, 41). Oxfam, CARE, World Vision and ECHO are all in the development category; they focus increasingly on integrated services, micro-finance, capacity-building, entrepreneurship, health and other development projects (Degnbol-Martinussen and Engberg-Pedersen 2005; Riddell 2008; Smillie 1997).

Other scholars have used other categories to distinguish NGOs, such as northern and southern NGOs, international NGOs (INGOs), transnational NGOs and local NGOs. The latter refers to small national NGOs that receive funding from larger northern NGOs.

Until 1980, there was a clear separation between humanitarian assistance and development. Development programmes were mostly carried out by the World Bank, the UN Development Program (UNDP), FAO, WHO, bilateral donors and other development-focused organizations (Degnbol-Martinussen and Engberg-Pedersen 2003). By the end of the 1980s, some NGOs began to shift their focus toward development as a way to soften the adverse consequences of structural adjustment programmes. This shift in NGO focus responded also to a shift in the architecture of international aid due to the neoliberal policies that began to be implemented in the 1980s. The NGOs that have become directly involved in development are generally known as development NGOs. Some examples of development NGOs are Oxfam, the Lutheran World Federation, CARE and World Vision. Their efforts include services that focus on economic, social and environmental sustainability, local participation, empowerment, ownership and micro-credit. The projects associated with such focuses have been known, whether genuinely effective or not, for their capacity to lift people out of poverty through service delivery and income-generating projects (Riddell 2008).

During the last three decades, development NGOs grew in size, relevance and outreach. Riddell (2008) estimates that the number of people directly benefiting from development NGOs was well over six hundred million in the early 2000s. Today, this number could be far higher. With the shift of official aid funding from governments to NGOs, it is argued that poor people in developing countries receive more assistance from NGOs' programmes and projects than those funded directly by official aid (Galway et al. 2012; Riddell 2008). In 2006, NGOs received more than US$2 billion in official development aid (Galway et al. 2012). According to the OECD, Official Development Assistance to the Third World totalled US$161.2 billion as the world was grappling with the COVID-19 crisis.[1] A large amount of this assistance was channelled through NGOs. However, the NGOs' contribution to development remains debatable. It has not been empirically proven that development goals can be reached only through the implementation of projects. Underdevelopment is a structural problem that needs to be addressed by appropriate policies, which start by tackling the underlying structural conditions that keep people in poverty.

Development is a complicated endeavour that requires a complex and multifaceted approach, which NGO projects alone cannot address. The main concern I have with development NGO projects is related to their sustainability. NGOs are wedded to neoliberal capitalist agendas that promote privatization, thus causing a drastic reduction of the role of the state and producing a strong confidence in the market. Pursuing this agenda makes their projects less about sustainability and more about filling the gaps left by the market (Galway et al. 2012; Schuller 2009). Studies have demonstrated how difficult it is for such projects to be sustained without consistent external support (Oakley and Floke

1999a; Riddell et al. 1999; Riddell 2008). Recounting an evaluation of the financial sustainability of NGOs, Riddell writes:

> The bulk of NGO evaluation material, which looks at the issue of sustainability, has concluded that most NGO projects are not financially sustainable without the continued injection of external funds. It is not surprising that the poorer the beneficiaries, the less likely they are to be able to pay for the services, training, and goods provided to them. Indeed, the prospects for financial sustainability of projects examined in the donor-funded study of Finished NGO-supported projects were judged to be so poor that it was suggested that many development projects were aptly called welfare projects as they consisted predominantly of helping poor people gain access to goods and services that they were unable to pay for themselves. (Riddell 2008, 281)

Alternatively, agenda-setting NGOs and local NGOs may attain more sustainable results as they are advocating for systemic policy changes. For example, studies support the notion that the work of human rights organizations has often led to changes in the law to protect land rights when lands have been appropriated (Landman and Abraham 2004; Roche 1999). Other successes have been attained in this area of agenda-setting. FUNCOL, a Colombian NGO, successfully worked for land rights for indigenous people (Carroll 1992). In Ghana, NGOs successfully promoted breastfeeding as an alternative to commercial milk powder (Chapman 2002). After the end of apartheid in South Africa, many NGOs showed a direct link between their activities and the end of apartheid. These results, which arise out of NGOs that are not primarily development-oriented, are more likely to increase capacity and produce development outcomes.

There is considerable evidence to assess the development impact and long-term structural change created by advocacy NGOs that focus on groups such as women and indigenous people. In Columbia, for example, NGOs such as Water for the People have been advocating for local community engagement in water issues during the last few decades. With the help of Water for the People, local NGOs in Cochabamba, such as *Agua Sustentable* (Sustainable Water) and *Fundación Abril* (April Foundation), implemented the eco-toilet project, through which they have designed new toilets using local materials and resources. This allows them to lower the cost of toilets from 420 to 250 bolivars (West 2014). Today, in many parts of Cochabamba, local cooperatives and other community-led groups manage their water resources. The result has seen a major improvement in access to water and sanitation in Cochabamba, as Madeline West (2014) has noted in her thesis, "Community Water and Sanitation Alternatives in Peri-Urban Cochabamba: Progressive Politics or Neoliberal Utopia".

At the local level, NGOs can also be crucial in increasing capacity and reducing people's vulnerability. In her study on NGOs in Haiti following the 2010 earthquake, Zanotti (2012) made a compelling argument about the effectiveness of local NGOs. In her ethnography of two community-based NGOs in Haiti, *Zanmi Lasante*[2] (Partners in Health) and Fonkoze, Zanotti concluded that the immediate impact of local NGOs on Haitian people's lives and reducing extreme poverty was more apparent than that of the larger northern NGOs.

Even at the local level, differences in NGOs' actions can be seen based on their funding source. For instance, Mark Schuller, an American anthropologist who conducted his dissertation research in Haiti, makes a distinctive observation between two local NGOs. They are of similar size and longevity and in the same line of intervention but with different donors. One NGO, Sove Lavi (Save Lives), receives funding from USAID, and the other local NGO, Fanm Tet Ansanm (Women United), receives most funding from private NGO donors. Schuller (2012) remarks that "whereas Sove Lavi repeatedly brushed aside member concerns in favour of top-down mandates, triggering local conflicts, Tet Ansam enjoyed relatively high levels of autonomy and member participation" (9). Schuller also concludes that according to donors, "Fanm Tet Ansam performed beyond expectations" (47) and that its interventions are more likely to bring long-term outcomes.

Linking Disaster Relief and Development (LDRD)

The link between relief and development gained greater importance at the end of the 1980s and into the 1990s. Particularly because of the sharply rising trend in natural disasters during the nineties, funding has become increasingly directed toward relief (Buchanan-Smith and

Maxwell 1994). In Africa and Asia, for example, relief efforts were spurred by growing numbers of emergencies in those regions due to an increase in natural disasters and a food security crisis (Christoplos 2006; O'Byrne 2013; Shipper and Pelling 2006). As a result, governments and donors increased their relief-assistance budgets. M. Buchanan-Smith and Simon Maxwell (1994) report that in southern Africa, relief budgets increased in the 1980s and 1990s. In Ethiopia, for example, the cost of relief was estimated to be 36 per cent of the national GDP when the country was hit by famine.

Furthermore, every donor with an extensive portfolio also sank more money into relief, such as Britain's ODA, which increased its relief budget from 2 per cent in 1982 to 12 per cent in 1992. The logic behind this increase was that if relief and development were implemented together effectively, they could provide people with secure livelihoods and safety nets capable of mitigating the frequency and impact of natural disasters. At the same time, it can ease the process of disaster rehabilitation (Buchanan-Smith and Maxwell 1994). Throughout the nineties, the discourse linking relief and development promoted a linear one-way transition from relief to development. This approach was known as the continuum model (Buchanan-Smith and Maxwell 1994; Christoplos 2006; Mosel and Levine 2014; Ramet 2012).

Linking relief and development through the continuum model proved to be very difficult because of the potential for relief to damage development efforts and increase people's vulnerabilities (Anderson and Woodrow 1998; Janse and Flier 2014; Ramet 2012). It became clear that in order for relief to reduce people's vulnerability, new instruments and approaches needed to be implemented. Scholars and aid agencies began to explore the *contiguum* approach that emphasized a "simultaneous and complementary use of different aid instruments" (Ramet 2012, 4). This model advocated for relief, rehabilitation and development to happen simultaneously. As a result, new concepts were invented, such as "sustainable recovery", "development-oriented relief", "disaster prevention and preparedness" and the like (Buchanan-Smith and Maxwell 1994; Ramet 2012). These were tools intended to, at least rhetorically, reshape the delivery of aid in an attempt to bridge the gap between the acute reaction to disaster and the long-term necessity of vulnerability reduction.

The *contiguum* approach proved also to be very complicated to put into practice. Part of this complication was due to the fact that disaster relief and development aid operated under two different umbrellas. In addition, there are fundamental differences between humanitarian assistance and development aid. They have different sets of goals and objectives. They also have different mandates, are governed by different principles and operate under different conditions and timeframes (Ramet 2012).

Also, concerns were being raised about the "grey zone", the funding gap between humanitarian assistance and development aid (Christoplos 2006; Mosel and Levine 2014). The long-term efforts aimed at reducing vulnerabilities and promoting development are often underfunded. In the case of post-earthquake intervention in Haiti, for example, Valerie Ramet (2012), in her "Policy Briefing to the European Parliament's Committee on Development," diagnosed a serious gap between EU emergency efforts in Haiti and its post-emergency intervention. She reported that the reconstruction was inadequately funded (Ramet 2012, 7).

In order to enhance LDRD, Ramet (2012) suggests a "better understanding between humanitarian and development actors, more funding and a reinforcement of existing coordination arrangements" (10). Bringing together humanitarian and development actors is an essential part of the resilience discourse (Mosel and Levine 2014; Otto and Weingärtner 2013). A focus on resilience argues for relief and rehabilitation to be integrated in ways that can produce long-term development outcomes. Following the simultaneous treatment approach, my research argues that for disaster aid to reduce vulnerability and produce long-term consequences, it needs to make development a centrepiece of its intervention by focusing on resilience. Development, in this context, must target the most vulnerable.

Theorizing Resilience in a Post-disaster Context

The concept of resilience became prominent in the UN's reports after the Hyogo World Conference on Disaster Risk Reduction. The conference was held less than a month after the Indian Ocean tsunami that spurred the creation of the Hyogo Framework for Action, which makes building disaster-resilient communities a development goal. In the Framework for Action, the argument was made that "disasters could be substantially reduced if people are well informed and motivated towards a culture of disaster prevention and resilience" (ISDR 2005, 9).

Building resilient communities requires a determination as to what makes that community vulnerable. As I argued earlier, vulnerability is caused – in addition to other factors – by poverty, income inequality, lack of employment, viable infrastructure and effective public safety policy. I define resilience as the social, economic and environmental factors that allow a community to withstand natural events and to recuperate when they occur quickly. Such factors include appropriate municipal infrastructure, protection of the environment, a robust public health care system, gender integration, increased financial capacities, promotion of education and disaster awareness, and policies to reduce risk and prepare for and respond to disasters. Resilience is not the absence of vulnerability. While vulnerability implies the incapacity of a community to withstand the effects of natural events or man-made disasters, resilience relates to the capacity of a community to mitigate and then quickly recover from the effects of an event. This nuance between resilience and vulnerability departs from John Twigg's approach that views resilience and vulnerability as "opposite sides of the same coin", which implies the more vulnerable a community is, the less resilient it is and vice versa (Twigg 2009, 3). Instead, I argue that vulnerability and resilience are on the same side of the coin in the sense that the more vulnerable communities can be the more resilient ones. In this way, in the face of vulnerabilities, resilience relates to the capacity to recover quickly. So, one does not indicate the other, but more vulnerabilities can make communities and people more resilient if they may have the capacity to recover quickly. Thus, resilience can function through capabilities for effective responses to disasters, even under conditions of vulnerability.

Building resilient communities largely depends on implementing policies and practices that enable vulnerable communities to withstand a disaster and facilitate recovery. With that in mind, as I explained earlier, a community that appears to be vulnerable may be more resilient than one that appears to be resilient in the first place. A comparison between Cuba and the United States proves that Cuba is much more resilient than the United States (Cuba is able to move its population out of harm's way) even though it may be more vulnerable in some respects (Lizarralde et al. 2014). For example, in September 2004, a tropical storm killed more than fifty people in the United States, while Cuba had no deaths. Hurricane Charley, also in 2004, caused the deaths of thirty people in Florida but killed only four people in Cuba. Hurricane Katrina killed more than one thousand eight hundred people in the United States, but no one was killed in Cuba, although the hurricane destroyed twenty thousand homes in the latter country (Lizarralde et al. 2014; Smith 2007).

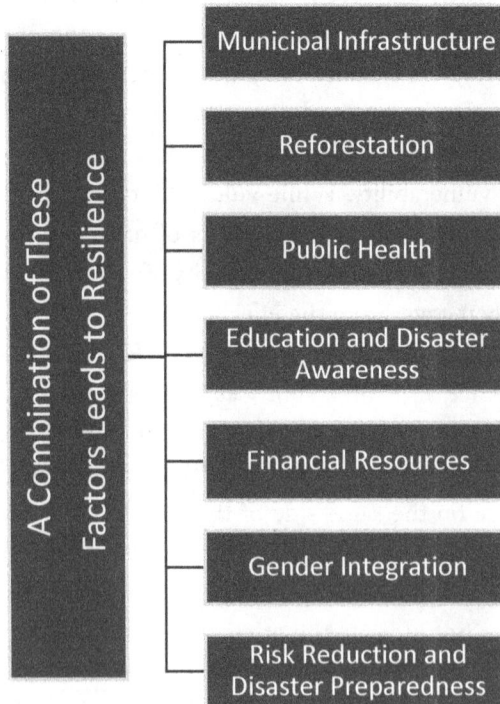

A Combination of These Factors Leads to Resilience

- Municipal Infrastructure
- Reforestation
- Public Health
- Education and Disaster Awareness
- Financial Resources
- Gender Integration
- Risk Reduction and Disaster Preparedness

Figure 2.2:   Resilience Indicators
Source: Figure Designed by the Author

Cuba's demonstrated resilience led the UNDP to propose Cuba as a "model" for disaster management and resilience in the Caribbean. "At the heart of the model is the promotion of local level decision-making that relies on coordinated early warning systems, risk and vulnerability studies, communications systems, effective database management and mapping, GIS, and community preparedness" (UNDP 2015). Based on that model, I propose a twofold approach that can build and strengthen resilience indicators to disaster and concurrently put in place sustainable development policies with an emphasis on disaster risk reduction management initiatives and community development.

The "resilience indicators" can help assess a community's level of resilience and can be acted upon to build a more resilient community. Below, I consider each indicator separately.

Municipal Infrastructure

Municipal infrastructure is one important determinant in building a resilient community. Developed countries adapt their infrastructure to hazards and risks. They do so with technology (Dore and Etkin 2003; Duffield 2010; Grove 2013, 2014; Reid 2012; Ward and Shively 2017). The most crucial aspect of such adaptation is determining how infrastructure was deficient prior to the damaging event. In developing countries, the majority of disaster-related damage stems from poor drainage systems, construction in high-risk areas, non-compliance with safety codes and inadequate road infrastructure that hinders timely first-aid response (World Bank 2003). Following a disaster, such vulnerable infrastructure should be identified, and resilience should be increased by enforcing new building codes and creating new infrastructure capable of withstanding or at least mitigating the consequences of future disasters. In other words, resilience depends on anticipating weaknesses and vulnerabilities and then taking measures to correct them in ways that can build capabilities to recover from the negative effects of disasters produced by existing vulnerabilities.

Reforestation

Floods are the most significant cause of disasters in the Caribbean (Meira and Phillips 2019; Kirton 2013), particularly in Haiti (Rencoret et al.

2010). Much of this risk can be attributed to deforestation. Numerous studies have shown that the presence of vegetation can significantly reduce the downstream transmission of flood waves and thus prevent catastrophic flooding events (Abernethy and Rutherfurd 2000; Brooks et al. 2003; Brooks and Brierley 2002; Hickin 1984; Thorne 1990). On top of this, a lack of riparian vegetation and human alteration of rivers can produce catastrophic erosion and landslides during large-magnitude floods (Brooks and Brierley 1997, 2000; Thompson and Croke 2013). Thus, we must ask the question: to what extent do deforestation and lack of vegetation contribute to disasters, and how can we build the ability to predict, anticipate and respond to catastrophic erosion, landslides and floods as a result of deforestation? And how is resilience built or increased at these levels?

Public Health

Public health refers to physical health infrastructures such as hospitals and clinics, as well as the management of health care systems and the efficacy of care (McEloy and Townsend 2015). Following a disaster, a robust public health system can facilitate the recuperation of its victims. It may also allow the community rehabilitation process to occur more rapidly. On the other hand, a weak public health system hinders the process of rehabilitation and may provoke subsequent disasters. When a disaster strikes, people often perish as a result not of the event but rather of inadequate health care. It has been observed that after a disaster, disease and infection tend to spread, and such conditions, if not managed properly, may lead to disastrous epidemics (Margaret et al. 2015).

After a disaster, critical questions must be asked: To what extent did the public health care system fail to save lives and prevent subsequent epidemics? And how can resilience be strengthened to avoid future health care crises? It is important to remember that health care infrastructure is costly, and limited resources can significantly hinder the construction or reconstruction of adequate facilities in the aftermath of a disaster. However, prevention is better than healing, so building health care resilience may begin first by prioritizing prevention, encouraging good hygiene health practices and developing food security. In this way, building resilience may require promoting primary care, building local clinics, training primary health care personnel and facilitating access to essential medications (Margaret 2015).

Education and Disaster Awareness

Education in this context refers to the standardization of disaster response (Anderson and Woodrow 1998). In times of crisis, survival instincts often cause people to make adverse decisions. Education and disaster awareness are intended to promote good practices and lay out the behaviours that are most effective both prior to and in the wake of a disaster. It aims to increase public understanding of risk, vulnerability and disaster reduction. It encompasses, for example, educating a population about seismic norms, respecting building codes, providing basic first aid and understanding the causes of natural disasters and the effects they might have on communities (Allen 2003; Anderson and Woodrow 1998; Bankoff 2008). Education, however, is not enough without public policies and proper legislation. Human beings will often engage in risky behaviours and enforce laws in order to set boundaries and limit adverse actions. Building effective resilience in this category first requires that we ask: in what way are people vulnerable due to a lack of disaster awareness, and how can we create conditions for people to learn and be prepared to withstand the next disaster?

Financial Resources

As I argued earlier, people are often vulnerable because of poverty, precarity and lack of financial resources. Lack of financial resources includes unemployment, limited access to credit, absence of protection against risk, savings depletion and lack of job security and insurance. The level of financial resources of an individual or a community closely aligns with the speed at which the individual or community will recover in the wake of a disaster. Building financial resilience requires necessary policies that the population can access during cases of financial institution collapse. In developed countries, people's livelihoods and properties are protected through diverse forms of insurance, retirement savings and government protection (Black and Evan 1999; Salt 2003). However, in some developing countries – like Haiti – populations are living without any form of protection against natural events, and thus, their livelihoods often vanish in the wake of disasters.

A lack of financial resources often constitutes one of the underlying factors in a disaster. Due to financial constraints, people construct houses in hazardous areas, use substandard materials and cut down trees for economic survival. When disaster strikes, they find themselves unable to cope or recover. To build a financially resilient community, we must ascertain the extent to which a population was financially vulnerable before the disaster. How was the financial vulnerability of the population evident? Furthermore, what structural factors contributed to this population's financial vulnerability?

Gender Integration

While natural events are not gendered, disasters are. The mere fact that an individual is a woman does not necessarily make her more vulnerable to any catastrophe or natural hazards (Bradshaw 1998). However, if vulnerability is frequently driven by a lack of resources, poverty, income loss and other material and socio-economic inequalities, then the fact that women are disproportionately affected by these conditions inherently makes them more vulnerable than men. Thus, vulnerability to an event is exacerbated by the subaltern position of women in a given society, and their disadvantage may influence how they perceive and respond to risk compared to men (Gustafson 998). As Bradshaw (2014) points out, the lack of information, education and engagement with preparedness activities that women face may limit their capacity to act when an event occurs. It, therefore, makes them more vulnerable and less resilient. Even after they survive a disaster, women (and particularly low-income women) face greater employment insecurity than their male counterparts (Bradshaw and Fordham 2013).

A successful relief effort needs to consider how women were disadvantaged before the event. To what extent did they participate in decision-making before the event? How did their economic conditions and lack of education impact their ability to act and respond to the catastrophic event?

Risk Reduction and Preparedness

Risk refers to "the probability of harmful consequences, or expected losses (deaths, injuries, property loss, livelihoods, economic activity disrupted or environment damaged) resulting from interactions between natural or human-induced disasters and vulnerable conditions" (UN 2004). This definition implies that exposure to hazards is not enough to put people at risk, but vulnerability is also a determining factor. Here, vulnerability involves the social, economic and environmental processes related to disaster response and recovery. There is a close relationship between risk reduction and disaster preparedness. Research has shown that disaster effects are mitigated when disaster awareness increases and early measures are taken – such as early warnings and temporary evacuation of people and property from hazard-prone areas – to ensure adequate response to the impact of hazards (Alexander 2013; Lizarralde et al. 2014, 2021; Twigg 2009). Disaster risk reduction (DRR) and preparedness require the development of a culture of safety and also that the public is informed on where to build and where not to, the rules of hygiene, the protection of the environment and the acceptance of shared responsibility and cooperation by community members. All these factors aim to reduce vulnerability to disaster while dealing with the conditions that trigger them in the first place (Twigg 2009).

However, the promotion of risk reduction measures and disaster preparedness is a matter of public policy accompanied by effective implementation. This requires a focus on development. As such, efficient relief efforts should integrate building resilience with a focus on effective DRR programmes. As Twigg argues, "there is very wide-ranging and there is potential and need for DRR initiatives in just about every sector of development and humanitarian work" (Twigg 2009, 9). Thus, DRR relates both to reducing vulnerabilities and building resilience. Both must go into policy, planning and practice.

Building Resilience through Disaster Relief: A Development Goal

Disaster relief, although intended to alleviate the suffering of disaster victims, can harm a community in the long run. It has been argued that the impact of disaster relief on a population can be as damaging as the original disaster (Anderson and Woodrow 1998). Because vulnerability precedes disaster and tends to increase after a disaster strikes, relief must be provided in ways that do not increase the severity of vulnerability but instead concurrently address it. If vulnerability is not addressed while providing relief, it may lead to future disasters. To ensure disaster relief efforts do not inadvertently increase vulnerability or weaken resilience, it is essential to prioritize development as a core objective.

Building resilience to disasters has been included in development discourses since the UN's 2005 report on the Hyogo World Conference on Disaster Reduction. It was understood that development, viewed as growth and accumulation, could cause vulnerability to disasters. The integration of resilience in development goals has opened new windows for sustainable development opportunities. The concept of sustainable development emerged from the Brundtland report *Our Common Future,* which defined sustainable development as "development that meets the needs of the present without compromising the ability of future generations to meet their own needs" (UN 1987).

Most recently, in 2015, the UN General Assembly adopted the 2030 "Agenda for Sustainable Development", which articulates a framework for peace and prosperity for people and the planet, now and in the future" (UN 2015). This framework targets seventeen sustainable development goals (SDGs), including good health and well-being, quality education, gender equality, good jobs and economic growth, clean water and sanitation, poverty reduction, and sustainable cities and communities. Effective disaster efforts must take those goals into account when delivering relief and building rehabilitation.

Promoting Development: The Role of NGOs

The concept of development has significantly evolved over the last few decades. Since World War II, its meaning has changed many times. Numerous scholars, mostly economists, have equated development with economic growth (Domar 1953; Horrod 1973; Kuznets 1971; 1973; Rostow 1960; Solow 1956). Walt Rostow (1960) is, particularly, well-known for this seminal approach that continues to influence people's perception of economic development. His theory of the five stages of economic growth,[3] published in 1960, was received as a prescription that low-income countries must follow to become developed. In fact, until today, the most common measure for economic development continues to be the gross domestic product index (GDP), which measures a country's national output and expenditure.

Economic growth is inescapably important to achieve development as it can lead to poverty eradication. Without growth, poor countries have fewer resources to invest in education, health and other infrastructure necessary for development (Goldin 2016). Yet development cannot be confined only to economic growth; it must also consider the social welfare of the people (Degnbol-Martinussen and Engberg-Pedersen 2003; Goldin 2016; Peet and Hartwick 2009; Sen 1999; Thorbecke 2006). Richard Peet and Elaine Hartwick (2007) write: "Development means creating a better life for everyone. In the present context of a highly uneven world, a better life for most people means, essentially, meeting basic needs: sufficient food to maintain good health, a safe, healthy place to live, affordable services available to everyone, and being treated with dignity and respect" (Peet and Hartwick 2007, 1). During the last decades, while some countries have not seen significant economic growth, they have managed to improve people's well-being. This is the case of many countries in West Africa, which, despite low GDP, have made improvements in education, health and life expectancy. Those social improvements are best articulated in terms of human development.

Human development theory especially argues against examining development only through the lens of economic growth. It assumes that GDP as a standard measure of economic growth failed to consider the true purpose of development, which consists of improving people's lives. It considers conditions of poverty and inequality that can be indubitably obfuscated by economic growth. Alternatively, it promotes well-being, a long and healthy life and access to education as indicators of development. Since 1990, those indicators have been featured in the United Nations Development Program's (UNDP) annual report as an alternative metric to rank countries' levels of development.

This human development idea is well echoed in Amartya Sen's (1999) influential book *Development as Freedom*. Sen's argument for development in this book is straightforward. Development is the substantive freedom that people must enjoy to live a full life. These freedoms can be optimized only when increasing individuals' capabilities to live the lives they have reason to value and to enhance their real-life choices (O'Hearn 2009). In a society where basic capabilities cannot be expanded for everyone, the individual's potential remains unfulfilled. For example, in his analysis of the cause of famine in his prior work, *Poverty and Famines: An Essay on Entitlement and Deprivation*, Sen (1981) claims that famine does not necessarily result from a lack of food but from the inequalities in food distribution mechanisms. Those inequalities often happen in non-democratic societies that forego expanding capabilities to a segment of the population when their entitlements to food have failed (Drèze and Sen 1991).

Although increasing income is one of the human capabilities, a focus on development as freedom recognizes that development is less about income and growth. Instead, it is mostly about the freedom for people to achieve a desired end with the income they have at their disposal. Having an income is not a guarantee of these substantive freedoms, which can be constrained by a lack of opportunities, societal violence, political instabilities and other social and political issues. This approach also recognizes the expansion of freedom both as the primary goal and as a principal means of development. Development, when viewed in this way, consists "of the removal of various types of unfreedoms, that leave people with little choice and opportunity of exercising their reasoning agency" (Sen 2000, xii). While Percy Hintzen (2019) agrees with Sen's approach to development as freedom, he argues that the realization of such freedom can be possible only under conditions of effective democracy and good governance. In his article, "Towards a New Democracy in the Caribbean: Local Empowerment and the New Global Order", Hintzen (2019), stresses that "in the West Indies the instrumentality of 'democratic governance' has systematically limited, constrained, and/or foreclosed the imperative of freedom and conditions for the realization of true development". Therefore, there is a need to transform the social and economic "processes" to produce more capabilities under the conditions of effective democracy freed from existing constraints.

This book draws on M. Anderson and P. Woodrow's (1999) approach that views development as the process by which capacities are increased and vulnerabilities decreased. "Vulnerability" is viewed here not only as social and cultural but also as physical and economic vulnerabilities. It refers to "a set of prevailing or consequential conditions composed of physical, socio-economic factors that adversely affect the ability to respond to events"[4] (Delica-Willison and Willison, 2004). Vulnerability is a more significant concern for the poor, as the poor are often the most vulnerable. Moreover, the social and cultural processes that foster vulnerability are primarily the products of international and national political economy (Cannon 1994).

Development both causes and prevents vulnerabilities. Analysing development through the lens of capacity and vulnerability provides insight into the relationship between NGOs (in their various forms) and development, as well as the differences in NGOs' actual and potential contributions to development, regardless of the type of actions in which they are engaged. I decided to focus on Haiti because of the extraordinary role NGOs play in every aspect of the country's functioning. NGOs are central to disaster relief in Haiti. Since the January 2010 earthquake, NGOs have been managing almost all disaster aid that the country has received.

Summary

In this chapter, I reviewed the scholarship on disaster relief, development and NGOs. Critical to this research is the distinction between extreme events and disasters. The former is the product of nature, and structural factors produce the latter. The possible transformation of hazards into disasters and, eventually, calamities is primarily contingent on the degree of development of the space where those events have occurred. Development, here, is not seen as growth and accumulation but rather as the process through which vulnerability is decreased and capacity for resilience is increased. I also reviewed the intensity of the scholarship on disaster relief, development and NGOs. Therefore, I emphasized that disasters often occur because of a lack of development and often affect the most vulnerable. My main argument, therefore, is that if disasters stem from a lack of development, disaster aid must be designed to foster development and enhance resilience to future disasters. In this context, disaster aid should serve as a gateway to development strategies that prioritize the needs of the most vulnerable.

THREE

Disaster Aid, NGOs and the Parallel State: Neoliberalism in Haiti and the Reliance on NGOs

For every complex problem, there is an answer that is clear, simple, and wrong.

H. L. Mencken

This chapter analyses the implementation of neoliberalism in Haiti. In the chapter, I consider two main phases of the implementation and the social and economic implications of each phase. The first phase provoked a depeasantization of the country. The second was marked by the privatization of most of the state-owned enterprises. Although this phase accelerated the urban migration that began in the first phase, the most pervasive consequence of the second phase was the weakening of the Haitian state.

The 1980s: The Beginning of the Depeasantization Process in Haiti

In the first phase of the implementation of neoliberalism in Haiti, particularly between 1986 and 1988, the United States (particularly USAID, along with the World Bank and the IMF) used their collective and significant influence to compel the Haitian government to open the country's economy to global capital and to eliminate import restrictions on goods and services (Dupuy 2005, 2014). This had devastating consequences for the Haitian economy even though in the initial phase of this process of liberalization, some jobs were created in the manufacturing sectors. It destroyed agricultural production and increased Haiti's food dependency, particularly on the United States.

Prior to 1985, the Haitian economy was based primarily on agriculture. The agricultural sector employed about 70 per cent of the active population and contributed 35 per cent to the country's GDP (Arthur 2002). By 1988, subsidized food from the United States flooded the Haitian market. For example, between 1986 and 1995, there was a dramatic increase in imports of rice from five thousand to nearly twenty thousand metric tons. This was also the case for sugar, coffee and other agricultural products (Dupuy 2014; Klarreich and Polman 2010).

Before 1960, Haiti was self-sufficient in its domestic food production (Moral 1961). The country began to suffer from declines in food production beginning in the 1960s even though, until the 1970s, domestic production contributed to most of the country's food supply. By 1981, Haiti was importing 23 per cent of the country's food supplies. These figures doubled during the 1990s and tripled in the 2000s. Today, about 80 per cent of the rice consumed in Haiti is imported from the United States (Dupuy 2014). Beginning in the 1980s, the average cost of imported food began to drop below that of locally produced food. Faced with lower-priced competition, Haitian peasants could no longer compete with food imported from the United States. This left them with two choices: leave the country altogether or migrate to urban areas (Charles 2002). Many Haitian peasants sold their land and joined an exodus from the country as waves of migrants – many using small and fragile boats – sought to immigrate to the United States. According to the US Immigration and Naturalization Service (INS), an estimated ninety-five thousand Haitians immigrated to the United States during the early 1980s. Thousands more perished at sea as they desperately tried to join other undocumented migrants (Charles 2002). Other farmers abandoned their land, and many of them migrated in masses to Port-au-Prince in search of manufacturing jobs. This rural-to-urban migration led to a process of depeasantization, as rural residents who were unable and unwilling to migrate overseas overwhelmed the cities and swelled their slums. The process of depeasantization was so significant that it exceeded the capacity of the growing manufacturing sector to absorb the vast majority of the displaced peasants. This confirmed Phillip McMichael's argument that "depeasantization does not itself create a global labour force; it simply swells the ranks of displaced people lacking needs of subsistence and needing wage work" (McMichael 2008, 96).

In the early 1980s, the manufacturing industry in Port-au-Prince could employ only sixty thousand people, though the population of the city rose substantially (Dupuy 1997). In 1971, the population of Port-au-Prince was estimated to be 493,932 (Microtrends 2020). In 1982, the population jumped to 763,188 (Microtrends 2020). Thus, Port-au-Prince's job market could not nearly accommodate the rapid influx of job seekers. This rapid urbanization and depeasantization was, however, a new phenomenon in Haiti. Up until 1989, Haiti had the lowest ratio of urban to rural population in the Caribbean and Latin America. With a population of over 6.1 million people in 1990, only 25 per cent lived in urban areas compared to 70 per cent in Latin America (Arsht 2014). This trend would reverse in the 1990s.

It is important to note that the destruction of agriculture also impacted the environment. As peasants could no longer compete with the imported food market, they began to cut trees to produce charcoal for economic survival. Charcoal has been Haiti's primary energy source to satisfy the energy demands of the rapidly growing urban population. This resulted in severe deforestation that caused excessive soil erosion and devastating floods. The latter has now become one of the most common weather-related catastrophes in Haiti (Singh and Barton-Dock 2015).

The 1990s: The Weakening of the Haitian State

The implementation of neoliberal policies in Haiti accelerated during the 1990s. In 1991, a leftist priest, Jean Bertrand Aristide, was democratically elected president of Haiti. Six months after he was sworn in, he was ousted from power by a military coup. After spending three years in exile in the United States, Aristide was returned to power by a US-led multinational force. During the years of military rule following the coup, development aid and programmes were put on hold, and an international economic embargo was placed on Haiti. The embargo had severe, devastating consequences for the country's economy. It resulted in the closure of most factories and assembly industries in Port-au-Prince, and nearly all the workers were laid off. The country's GDP fell by 26 per cent (Dupuy 2014). This put the country in desperate need of overseas economic assistance.

President Jean Bertrand Aristide returned to office on 15 October 1994. As a main condition of his return, "Aristide was compelled to accept the Emergency Economic Recovery Program (EERP) devised in Washington by a multinational task force of the IDB, the World Bank, the IMF, and the USAID" (Dupuy 2014, 57). The EERP was a reformulation of former neoliberal policies. Because of parliamentary opposition and widespread protests, Aristide was not able to implement the policies. As a result, the international community withheld aid to his government but increased NGO funding.

In 1996, René Préval, Aristide's former prime minister, became president. He found himself in desperate need of international aid[1] and was pressured by the IFIs to implement the EERP. In October 1996, Préval agreed, on behalf of the government, with the World Bank and the IMF to undertake the following reforms: 1) reduce tariffs for foreign companies, 2) reduce the size of public services, 3) privatize state-owned enterprises, 4) grant tax benefits to private capital (for example, exempting it from taxation for three years) and 5) create enclave industrial areas (Etienne 1997, 86).

The World Bank praised this agreement, proclaiming that "the government has made significant efforts to maintain macroeconomic stability, which need to be continued and strengthened" (Dupuy 2005, 61). By 1999, some prominent public enterprises were privatized, and international tariffs were either reduced or eliminated. The privatization of state-owned enterprises in Haiti was intended to open the country up to foreign direct investment for export production, but instead, it increased the country's dependency.

Many of the state-owned enterprises that were privatized were profitable, or potentially profitable, at the time of their privatization (Crémieux 1996; Dupuy 2015). For example, one company, Haiti

Cement (Le Ciment d'Haiti), produced between two hundred and fifty thousand to four hundred and fifty thousand tons of cement per year before it was privatized. During the 1980s, the company boomed, transferring about 42 per cent of its profits to the public treasury. However, the embargo that was placed on Haiti from 1991 to 1994 forced it to close down.

The embargo on Haiti and the decision to lift it can be explained by a convergence of political and economic interests on the part of the United States. It was initially imposed for punitive political reasons but was rescinded under the imposed neoliberal conditionalities that drove US foreign policy, and the government of Haiti agreed to that. These imposed conditionalities provided US investors with the opportunity to acquire profitable Haitian enterprises. A typical example is The Minoterie d'Haiti, a flour company that was forced to close in 1992 during the embargo. At the time, the company was producing between one hundred and thirty-five thousand and one hundred and fifty thousand tons of flour per year and was highly profitable. Between 1980 and 1990, 90 per cent of its profits were transferred to the public treasury. In June 1997, after the embargo was lifted, the company was sold to two US multinational companies (Continental Grain Company and Seaboard Corporation) and one Haitian company (SNI Minoterie SA, a subsidiary of the UNIBANK, a private bank in Haiti). This was the typical fate of many other public enterprises that were sold under Preval's administration from 1996 to 2001.

The purchase of local companies was a strategy employed by foreign interests to use their infrastructure as a springboard to gain control of the country's economy. This was achieved to the detriment of local workers who were laid off. Many of the acquired companies were closed, and their sites were used as warehouses for imported food products. In 2001, because of its neoliberal policies, Haiti became recognized as one of the most open and liberal markets in Latin America (Bazin 1990).[2]

The agreement to accept neoliberal policies by the Haitian government was partly secured through the withholding of badly needed aid, both under the Aristide presidency and at the beginning of Préval's. Nonetheless, direct assistance provided to the Haitian government declined significantly even after the implementation of neoliberal policies. The IMF, the World Bank and the United States instead shifted funding to NGOs. Marc Bazin, former Minister of Planning and Cooperation during the 1990s, wrote:

> The liberalization effort has taken place virtually without a decent level of international aid, and Haiti has paid a very high price for its foray into globalization, given, in particular, the inadequacy of human and physical resources, as reflected in particular, in higher unemployment, reduced purchasing power, greater inequalities, and low per capita food production. (Bazin, as cited in Dupuy 2014, 62)

The demographic impact of Haiti's liberalization programme was also significant as the process of depeasantization continued to accelerate. From 1995 to 2000, the population of Port-au-Prince (the greater Port-au-Prince area) increased from 1.427 million to 1.693 million (Microtrends 2020). This trend continued throughout the 2000s, at a rate of seventy-five thousand people per year (USAID 2007). At the time of the 2010 earthquake, Port-au-Prince had 2.643 million residents (Microtrends 2020), which represented 25 per cent of the country's total population (HISI 2014; Zanotti 2010). Without formal employment, most of the population was earning their livelihood from the informal economy, which employs more than 80 per cent of the Haitian workforce and relied on remittances from the Haitian overseas diaspora. NGOs provided most public services at the time.

My argument thus far is that neoliberalism produced depeasantization and destroyed the domestic production of goods and services, especially domestic food production. Haiti moved from food self-sufficiency to dependence on imported food. Urban manufacturing was unable to absorb displaced rural labour, contributing to massive outmigration, dependence on the informal economy and reliance on an influx of remittances from abroad. Neoliberalism also reduced the government's capacity to cater to the needs of the population, leading to dependence on NGOs.

Privatization was described by the International Financial Institutions (IFIs) as a recipe to strengthen macroeconomic stability, encourage private sector investment and increase productivity. As the World Bank report *Haiti: The Challenges of Poverty Reduction* stated:

Boosting private investment will provide the underpinnings of Haiti's future economic growth. A first important step will be the implementation of the capitalization program, telecommunications, electricity, water sector, ports, and airports. Privatization of these sectors would increase the productivity of the economy and provide a clear signal as to the Government's commitment to redefining the role of the state and set the economy on a modern course. The Government has made significant efforts to maintain macroeconomic stability, which needs to be continued and strengthened. (World Bank 1998, vii)

However, at the same time, the report highlighted the impact of such policies on the capacity of the state to invest in social programmes for the poor. The bank recommended that the NGO sector provide the services that were part of the functions of the state. The bank wrote:

A huge challenge for the Haitian state will be increasing resources allocated to the finance of social service provision. In education, health, water and sanitation, and family planning, Government should continue to leave the delivery of these services to the private and/or NGO sectors to the maximum extent possible, while the government itself strives to improve the regulatory framework, facilitate coordinated efforts among its activities, those of private actors, and the poor themselves. Limited government resources should be directed at programs that are targeted to the very poor, particularly those in rural areas which have been neglected in the past. Until the benefits of these longer-term investments in human capital are felt, the existence of targeted transfers and social safety net programs will continue to be important to the survival of the Haitian population. (1998, vii)

The benefits expected from the implementation of these liberalization policies have yet to be realized. Instead, poverty continues to persist in Haiti. The per capita income that was US$632 in 1980 fell by US$332 in 2003 (Verner 2007). Haiti entered the 2000s with disappointing GDP growth of 0.7 per cent in 2000, followed by two years of negative growth of 1.04 per cent in 2001 and 0.25 per cent in 2001. There was a slight increase to 0.36 per cent in 2003 (World Bank 2020), yet extreme poverty remained. In 2001, 49 per cent of the population, totalling 3.9 million people, was living under conditions of extreme poverty (Verner 2007). These were the conditions at the time when NGOs had begun to take over almost all government services.

The Proliferation of NGOs in Haiti

The proliferation of NGOs in Haiti occurred in two waves. The first wave occurred during the 1980s, triggered by humanitarian concerns and concerns over government corruption. The second wave occurred during the 1990s and 2000s, triggered by declines in state capacity due to the implementation of neoliberal policies in Haiti. During this period, the proliferation became significant and produced a shift to complete reliance on NGOs.

The First Wave and the Increased Presence of NGOs in Haiti

NGOs have been providing services in Haiti since the 1950s. The Cooperation for American Relief Everywhere (CARE) and the Catholic Relief Service (CRS) were among the first NGOs that began to deliver services in Haiti and were followed by a few Christian NGOs in the 1960s. During the 1970s and 1980s, the number of NGOs began to increase in Haiti (Etienne 1997; Louis 2012).

In 1971, Jean Claude Duvalier succeeded his father, Francois Duvalier, as president of Haiti. The young president pledged to engage the country in economic progress. While his policies benefited the political and economic elites, most of the population sunk into poverty, and many fell into starvation (Charles 2002; Trouillot 1987). This led to an eruption of food riots at the beginning of the 1980s.

The escalation of poverty and starvation attracted international attention, particularly in the wake of an exodus of Haitians attempting to migrate by sea during what came to be known as the "boat people crisis". Many of them died in the attempt. This loss of human lives troubled the international public. Extensive media coverage of the situation led NGOs to increase their presence in Haiti, while the United States and European countries increased financial assistance (Etienne 1997).

Because of the Haitian government's well-deserved reputation for corruption, the international community bypassed the state and provided aid directly to NGOs for distribution to the people. In 1988, in their article "The Challenge of Administrative Reform in Post-Duvalier

Haiti: Efficiency, Equity and the Prospects for Systemic Change", Brinkerhoff and Goldsmith wrote:

> Faced with a national administrative network that lacked modern skills and was riddled with corruption, most external agencies in Haiti in the 1970s and 1980s chose to work around the central administration, either by collaborating with NGOs or by setting up autonomous public bodies over which they could exercise close oversight. (14)

The trend of bypassing the government continued, even after the fall of Jean Claude Duvalier in 1986. However, until the end of the 1980s, the number of NGOs operating in Haiti remained relatively low. According to the 1987 World Bank report, the number of NGOs in Haiti was estimated to be three hundred. More significant increases occurred during the 1990s.

The Second Wave and the Shift to a Complete Reliance on NGOs

In 1997, Sauveur Pierre Etienne published his book, *Haiti: The Invasion of NGOs*, to bring public attention to the increased presence of NGOs in Haiti. He estimated the number of NGOs working in Haiti at the time to be eight hundred. During the decade of the 2000s, the proliferation increased significantly. By the time of the 2010 earthquake, the number of NGOs operating in Haiti had risen to roughly ten thousand[3] (Klarriech and Polman 2012), giving Haiti the second-highest number of NGOs per capita in the world, following India.

The rapid increase of NGOs in the 1990s and the 2000s was symptomatic of a larger phenomenon. At the global level, international donors have begun to circumvent Third World countries' governments and to increase their funding for NGOs. The 1990s saw a sevenfold increase in NGO's official aid funding worldwide, from US$1 billion in 1970 to US$7 billion in 1990 (Ahmed and Potter 2006). As funding was funnelled into NGOs, their global presence rose rapidly, from six thousand NGOs in 1990 to an estimated sixty thousand in 1998 (Reagan 2003, 3).

Two fundamental underlying reasons can explain the increase in official aid to NGOs and the global increase in their numbers: an international debt crisis and the neoliberal policies that began to be implemented in the 1980s. As a response to a significant increase in the amount of foreign and national debt held by countries in the global south, the IFIs imposed structural adjustment regimes on indebted countries under strict conditionalities that had the effect of significantly changing state social priorities (McMichael 2008). NGOs were seen as alternatives to the state based on the argument that they were more cost-effective and better equipped to reach the poor (Lewis 2006; Ahmed and Potter 2006). With neoliberal policies demanding a reduced role of the state, NGOs were compelled to step in and fill the gap (Drabek 1987; Galway et al. 2012; Schuller 2009).

The increase of NGOs in Haiti followed a global trend spurred by neoliberalization. Its implementation in the 1990s led to the almost total collapse of the state and a heavy reliance on NGOs. As the country came to rely almost exclusively on NGOs, they became increasingly influential players in its political economy.

NGOs in Haiti: The Construction of a Parallel State

In the wake of neoliberalism, scholars such as Aihwa Ong, James Ferguson and Michel-Rolph Trouillot have questioned the constitution of the state and its relationship to national governance. Particularly, Trouillot (2001) has observed in the context of globalization that the state has become fragmented and diffused. Trouillot's argument is not an absolute assertion that national governments are no longer relevant. However, their functions have been transformed into the service of global capital as they provide the necessary legalities and authorize the presence of transnational processes and practices. "State effects" are made possible through the national government apparatus as well as, particularly in the global south, powerful international institutions. Percy Hintzen defines state effects as "the actual effects of the processes and practices of power on the material lives of people and their subjectivities, exercised either directly in the deployment of the technologies of global power or indirectly through the authority of the national apparatus of governance" (Hintzen 2020, 185). When considering the increased relevance of NGOs in the global south as it relates to the fragmentation of the state power, the question I then posit is: What is left of the role of the state in developing countries?

To begin to answer, I want to point to the shift in the architecture of aid and the way this has profoundly changed the mission of NGOs during the last two decades. After World War II and until the 1970s, the mission of NGOs was fundamentally humanitarian (Pierre-Louis 2011; Riddell 2008). By the 1980s, however, they began to become engaged in other activities, including development. Kim D. Reimann, in his 2006 article "A View from the Top: International Politics, Norms and the Worldwide Growth of NGOs", notes that before 1988, only 6 per cent of World Bank development projects were implemented through NGOs. By early 1990, this number rose to 30 per cent. During the late 1990s, 50 per cent of World Bank projects were implemented through NGOs (Reimann 2006, 49). With the UN's reduction of poverty agenda and sustainable development goals, NGOs have become even more engaged in development and poverty reduction. Increasingly, funders and development agencies are shifting their funding allocations to NGOs (Reimann 2006).

In Haiti's case, as neoliberal policies became more extensively implemented during the 1990s and early 2000s, aid increasingly shifted to NGOs. This shift increased their relevance and influence in such a way that some scholars, most notably Mark Schuller (2007, 2012), have portrayed them as functioning as a "parallel state". In his book *NGOs in Haiti: Killing with Kindness*, Schuller makes this observation:

> The earthquake exposed the weakness of the state ... The state has no ability to prevent the disaster or coordinate the relief efforts. The government had been weakened since the mid-1990s by donor's policies of giving their aid directly to NGOs. Even before the earthquake, more than 80 per cent of the health clinics and 90 per cent of schools were private, run by individuals, missions, and NGOs-particularly the large food distribution agencies like World Vision, CARE (Cooperative for American Relief Everywhere), or Catholic Relief Services-became parallel states, even marking off territory into their area. (Schuller 2012, 6)

There is a great deal of discussion about the relevance of the state in the age of globalization, as mentioned earlier. The Haitian anthropologist Michel-Rolph Trouillot has attempted to explore the transformational role of the state during the last decades. In his seminal work, *The Anthropology of the State in the Age of Globalization: Close Encounters of a Deceptive Kind*, Trouillot distinguishes the state from national government. He depicts the state not as a site or an apparatus of government but rather as a "set of processes and practices" (Trouillot 2001, 130). Based on his unconventional approach, he points out what he identifies as a displacement – a move away from the national power in the age of globalization. He argues that state power is diffused and transferred beyond the site of national governments as other institutions begin to act in a state-like manner. Trouillot writes, "State-like processes and practices also obtain increasingly in nongovernmental sites such as NGOs or trans-state institutions such as the World Bank. These practices, in turn, produce state effects as powerful as those of national governments" (Trouillot 2001, 130).

James Ferguson (2006) makes a similar observation in pointing to the emergence of new forms of government through NGOs and transnational networks. In the case of Africa, Ferguson points out that humanitarian organizations such as Oxfam, CARE, or Doctors Without Borders perform state-like functions (Ferguson 2006). He argues that those organizations do not replace the state, which has far from disappeared. He affirms that they act unquestionably in a state-like manner in many aspects. Trouillot (2002) further affirms that nongovernmental sites such as NGOs or trans-state institutions such as the World Bank produce state effects that are even more powerful than national governments.

Suppose I place my question in the context of the heavy presence of powerful NGOs in developing countries, and thus transnational corporations, the IFIs and bilateral control of their economies and other multilateral presences. In that case, it is no exaggeration to assert that the national government in many developing countries has become a "shadow state". The concept "shadow state" was used initially by William Reno (1999) to reference the way officials in the weak states of Africa gained power through concealed alliances with warlords, arms traders, and multinational firms instead of through more formal processes used by Western democracies (Ferguson 2006; Reno 1999). In a general sense, the word "shadow" describes a doubling – a copy of something real (Ferguson 2006, 16). Likewise, and for the same reasons, Georges Fouron (2001) considers Haiti to be an apparent state, which implies that the primary functions of governance are other powerful forces, such as influential international NGOs.

NGOs cannot replace the state. Whether a shadow or an apparent entity, the national government will continue to be consequential in many aspects as it continues to maintain what Hintzen calls "strategies for regime survival" through the use of ideology, patronage, control and coercion (Hintzen 1998, 10–12). Regimes use the national apparatus of governance to control many functions, such as the military and police, constitutionality and legality, legislation, the judiciary, etc. My argument is that, as a consequence of neoliberalism, some processes and practices were formerly the purview of state function that have been taken over, for reasons I have discussed above, by other entities, both local and international.

In the case of NGOs in Haiti, they have not replaced the state. However, I see them as parallel structures that perform certain state functions that have been abandoned because of the state's inability to cater to the needs of its population. I characterize the NGOs in Haiti as a parallel state. Such considerations have political and economic implications. Among these, the most important is related to the reality that 1) NGOs have more access to international transfer than the Haitian state, 2) they provide more services than the state and 3) they exercise considerable influence over the government.

1.   NGOs Have More Capacity Than the State

The access to international transfers of funds by NGOs in Haiti has increased since the 1990s, when international donors decided to fund them directly, bypassing the government. This trend continued into the 2000s, persisting after the 2010 earthquake. In 2004, USAID pledged US$1.2 billion to Haiti, the vast majority of which was disbursed through NGOs (Hallward 2007). At the International Donors' Conference after the earthquake, donors pledged US$5.3 billion to Haiti to be disbursed in two years. However, only 1 per cent of the fund was channelled through the national government (Klarreich and Polman 2010).

2.   NGOs Provide More Services Than the State

Due to the large sum of money at their disposal, NGOs provide services that the state would otherwise provide. Before the 2010 earthquake, 72 per cent of Haiti's basic health care services were delivered by NGOs. They also provided 80 per cent of primary education, sanitation, and water provision (Hallward 2007; International Crisis Group 2009; Zanotti 2010). NGOs also operate in the agricultural, infrastructural, and housing sectors. Finally, NGOs are reaching out to people in remote areas of the country where there is no governmental presence at all. In those areas, they engage through community organizations and act in a state-like manner.

This is primarily the result of the inefficiency of the national government, which removes itself from the responsibility and the burden of catering to the needs of the population. This same argument can also be made for remittances. Generally governments in Haiti have encouraged the country's overseas communities to send remittances. These exceed foreign exchange earnings from foreign direct investments, foreign aid, grants and export earnings. Members of the diaspora organize themselves to help their communities and intervene where the national government failed. Moreover, the national government has adapted to this reality.

3.   NGOs Control the Government's Actions or Operate Outside of the Government

NGOs exercise a form of control over some of the government's social programmes and infrastructure decisions. Following the earthquake, with billions of dollars of reconstruction aid, NGOs constructed a powerful structure of operations and intervention. Many government projects have been oriented and financed by NGOs. The stage for this form of control was set even before the earthquake. Francois Pierre-Louis (2011), in his article "Earthquakes, Nongovernmental Organizations, and Governance in Haiti", reports that even before the earthquake, there was a parallel NGO for every ministry that executed programmes and projects. Decisions were often made on the type of projects to finance without the Haitian government's knowledge and consent. Pierre-Louis (2012) indicates that in 2007, for example, USAID, one of Haiti's biggest donors, distributed funds directly to NGOs and assigned specific NGOs to specific ministries to execute specific projects.[4] When they are not orienting government actions in that way, they simply operate outside of any government control. They decide what their priorities are and the domain and length of their intervention. They self-evaluate their projects and decide for themselves how, where and when to allocate funding. They are only accountable to donors who can withdraw their funding.

There is a case to be made that NGOs also have a vested interest in catering to the needs of their officials and institutional needs. They also contribute to the production and reproduction of a domestic elite. They provide the latter with significantly more prestige, income and authority than working for the government. They exercise influence and power, grant access to visas and offer opportunities to travel and participate in relevant meetings in diverse countries. NGOs' offices are better equipped than governmental offices. Their employees work in spaces similar to those in the Western industrialized metropolis. They enjoy many amenities, including air-conditioning, computers and internet access. NGO officials often have chauffeurs, drive nicer vehicles and earn better salaries than their government counterparts. NGOs hire the most educated people in the country, and those well-paid employees represent what Mark Schuller (2007, 2012) calls the "NGOs class", a group of high-income earners who are benefiting from privileges inaccessible to the majority of the Haitian population. This class comprises not only Haitians but also international workers and organizational officials from countries where they are headquartered or where their donors are located. They live in large modern houses in wealthy areas of Haiti. This is because they are donor-dependent (Pierre-Louis 2012) upon funders integrally tied to the United States, Canada and European Union economies to which their job security is tied. The interests of the countries in which they are located are not necessarily paramount.

Furthermore, they form an integral part of the neoliberal agenda and its imperatives. This may partly explain why NGO projects often address the symptoms of problems instead of the structures that produce them. They may have a vested interest in perpetuating them.

Summary

In this chapter, I critically examine the political and economic factors that contribute to Haiti's heavy reliance on NGOs. Among those factors, I highlighted the neoliberal policies implemented in Haiti during the 1980s and 1990s and argue that neoliberalism disrupted an economy that was based on domestic production and local public and private ownership. The result was depeasantization as well as foreign ownership and control through liberalization policies. The latter reduced state capacities and capabilities, which led to dependence on NGOs to perform functions that the national government previously assumed. This was in keeping with global processes linked to transnationalization. Haiti was particularly vulnerable because of the influence of external actors even before the implementation of neoliberalism. It was also rendered vulnerable because of a history of corrupt governance that catered almost exclusively to the interests of the upper strata who were closely aligned to Western, especially American, capitalist interests.

FOUR

Political Instability, Underdevelopment and (Un)Natural Disasters in Haiti Before the 2010 Earthquake

> Those controlling political power will eventually find it more beneficial to use their power to limit competition, to increase their share of the pie, or even to steal and loot from others rather than support economic progress.
>
> *Daron Acemoğlu, author of* Why Nations Fail: The Origins of Power, Prosperity and Poverty

There are structural factors related to conditions of postcolonial governance and Haiti's colour-and-class-based stratification order that have contributed to the country's vulnerability to disasters and its relative and differential capacities for resilience. The January 2010 earthquake was a human-made disaster. It stemmed from the consequences of political and economic choices made decades before. It also resulted from the ineptitude of a political system that robbed (and has continued to rob) the vast majority of the Haitian population of development and progress. The calamities the country faced following the 2010 earthquake, which captured global attention, are merely symptoms of deeper, underlying issues. The theoretical framework that I employ to analyse these issues combines a critical understanding of Percy Hintzen's work on the costs of regime survival with an awareness of the tension between the state and the nation from the perspective of Michel-Rolph Trouillot's *Haiti: State Against Nation.*

The Costs of Regime Survival

In his seminal work, *The Costs of Regime Survival: Racial Mobilization, Elite Domination and the Control of the State in Guyana and Trinidad,* Percy Hintzen (1998) critically investigates the conflict that political leaders in underdeveloped countries face between sacrificing the collective needs of the society and serving the interests of the elites. The book focuses particularly on Guyana and Trinidad, both countries that obtained their independence during the second half of the twentieth century. In the book, Hintzen laid out three fundamental needs that a post-independence regime may face if they are to survive: 1) the need to satisfy or neutralize powerful local and international actors, 2) the need to demobilize and co-opt the organized opposition and 3) the need to retain mass support and prevent outbidding (Hintzen 1998, 9–10).

To meet those conditions, Hintzen points out five strategies that political leaders in less-developed countries often utilize:

1. *Ideology.* According to Hintzen, ideology – particularly what he called "practical ideology" – refers to socio-political programmes that political leaders organize to communicate with both local and international actors. Ideology can vacillate when it is necessary for leaders to gain and maintain control of resources from local international actors. Political leaders or statesmen can also change ideology in the face of new demands as these relate to changes in domestic and international landscape, specifically when those changes are more likely to threaten their power.

2. *Patronage.* This refers to the distribution of state resources in exchange for political support. Through patronage, political leaders develop clientelistic ties with elites in exchange for their support. Patronage can also be used to gain mass support or control members of the military and security forces or even political leaders from the Opposition.

3. *Control.* To expand activities under the domain of the state bureaucracy, political leaders use control. Control, in this context, is employed to deprive political opponents of their

resources. Control can be maintained, for example, through nationalization of the economy, deactivation and infiltration of trade union organizations, swaying the legislative process to support the government, placing political agents in key positions in the administration, centralizing the state bureaucracy, etc.

4. *Coercion.* This refers to the utilization of the state apparatus against political opponents, dissident groups or any segments of the population that intend to engage in activities against the government. Coercion, according to Hintzen (1998), proved to be the most effective and efficient strategy that political regimes utilize for their survival.

5. *International Realignment.* As regimes in less developed countries face local and national threats, they also face international threats that can jeopardize their survival. When facing international threats, regimes can often seek alternative suppliers for resources that are essential to their survival. Those resources include material resources as well as military resources to guarantee their defence against powerful countries (Hintzen 1998, 10–12).

While Hintzen's *The Costs of Regime Survival* was a case study of Guyana and Trinidad, it may also apply to Haiti.

The State Against Nation

The term "state against nation" was coined by Michel-Rolph Trouillot in his book *Haiti: State Against Nation: Origins and Legacy of Duvalierism.* The term serves to highlight the extreme disjuncture between the state and the nation under the regime of Duvalier in Haiti. In his argument, Trouillot rejected the "mainstream conception of the nation as a cultural construct that offers some claim to homogeneity in relation to political power" (Trouillot 1990, 25). Investigating the case of Haiti, he argued that there has always been a structural division between the Black Creole-speaking population (peasantry that constituted the nation) and the upper strata who controlled governance (who were French-speaking and depended upon global interests).

During the nineteenth century, the Haitian nation was divided into two groups: the peasantry and the urbanites. The peasantry, although representing the majority of the population, was considered *peyi andeyo*,[1] or part of "something outside the country". The peasants were called *moun andeyo*, or "people outside" (Trouillot 1990). The urbanites mainly represented the urban population of Port-au-Prince, dominated by a French-speaking elite. The urbanites comprised the following groups:

1.   The upper class, mostly mulattoes and light-skinned individuals. They were predominantly businessmen and landowners.

2.   The petite bourgeoisie and the upper-middle class, made up partially of educated Black elite professionals, bureaucrats of public sectors, high ranking military officers, etc.

3.   The middle class and lower-middle class – mostly small business owners, primary and secondary schoolteachers, skilled workers and soldiers. Trouillot (1990) identified them as a parasite group that depended on the public sector for a job. Without the state, the middle class could not reproduce themselves.

4.   Finally, the lower class, composed of artisans, day labourers, small vendors, maids, servants, etc. (Pierre-Charles 1973; Trouillot 1990).

The social and spatial division between the two factions of the country, the rural and the urban or the peasants and the urbanites, had cultural, economic and political implications. The peasants were mostly illiterate, and they did not speak French, the official language at that time , and the language of the elites. Thus, the urbanites used language to culturally and politically isolate the peasants and exclude them from the political process while maintaining a necessary symbiotic economic relationship. The peasants brought their goods to urban markets, and they brought back necessities that were not available in the hinterland to their villages. These economic transfers between the peasants and the urbanites continued for most of the twentieth century (Trouillot 1990). Through those transfers, the state extracted surplus revenues from the peasantry through taxes that they were forced to pay.

Trouillot explained that both the peasants and the urbanites were conscious of the split between them. As he put it:

> The Haitian expression *moun andeyo* (literally, "people outside") that urbanites use to describe the peasantry is as telling as the *l'arrière-pays* ["the hinterland"]. It signifies both an acknowledgment and an implicit approval of the split. Few urbanites ever wondered how a majority of the nation could be seen as being "outside." Peasants in turn often refer to powerful individuals, especially urbanites, as *leta* ("the state"), regardless of their actual ties to the state apparatus. In short, both sides acknowledge that a split exists. (1990, 81)

The peasants were poor and illiterate. The 1950s census reported that 89.5 per cent of the population was illiterate (Pierre-Charles 1973, 34), many of whom were peasants. The functioning of the urban strata largely depended on the surplus extracted from the peasantry and through taxes. The US occupation of Haiti from 1915 to 1934 reinforced the split between the state and the nation. It did so by worsening the socio-economic contradictions between the peasantry and the urbanites, which consequently contributed to greater marginalization of the peasantry. Proponents of the occupation often point to the infrastructural improvements that the country had undergone during that time (Ferguson 1987). In fact, many infrastructural improvements were made while it was in effect. However, those improvements reinforced a more centralized system. During the occupation, Port-au-Prince became the centre of almost everything. Government administration offices, hospitals, schools and new infrastructures were concentrated in Port-au-Prince (Charles 2002; Ferguson 1987; Trouillot 1990). The peasantry gained nearly nothing from the infrastructural improvements undertaken during the occupation (Ferguson 1987).

The US occupation also reinforced the disjuncture between the state and the nation through a process of "whitening" the state apparatus. Colour prejudices that existed before the occupation were aggravated. Mulattoes, or light-skinned Haitians from the elite classes, were placed in positions of authority, mostly apart from the very few dark-skinned Haitians who occupied important positions in the ministries and army (Trouillot 1990).

During the occupation, the peasantry was encumbered with a heavy tax burden, particularly through the export of coffee. At this time, coffee became the most important export commodity in Haiti, accounting for

74 per cent of all exports. By the end of the occupation, customs duties represented more than 80 per cent of government revenue (Trouillot 1990, 103). Those figures inform us of the extent to which the peasantry was being exploited during the occupation.

However, it was under the Duvaliers (Papa Doc and Baby Doc) that the disjuncture between the state and the nation (the political and the civil society) became exacerbated. Francois Duvalier was a dark-skinned politician. Along with Jean Price Mars, Jacques Roumain and other Haitian intellectuals, he was an advocate of the cultural and political philosophy of *négritude,* which advocated for the rehabilitation of the Black race in the Caribbean and francophone Africa (Charles 2020). His version of *négritude* came to be known as *noirisme,* which promoted Black middle-class power.

Duvalier was a physician who had a history of working with the peasantry. He was known for treating the poor in rural areas and fighting against the spread of infectious diseases. The peasants loved him and passionately called him Papa Doc (Haggerty 1991). In 1946, he was appointed general director of Public Health in Haiti. He rose from that position to become president of Haiti in 1957 and, in April 1964, declared himself president for life with the right to nominate his successor. He remained in power until his death on 21 April 1971. He was succeeded by his son, Jean Claude Duvalier, who became known as "Baby Doc", assuring the continuity of the regime.

In analysing the Duvalierist regimes (Papa Doc's and Baby Doc's), Trouillot points to three of its characteristics: extreme violence, incompetence and corruption. While Haiti has had a long history of state violence and dictatorship, under Papa Doc Duvalier it became notably and qualitatively distinct from that of previous dictators. In the process, Duvalier amplified the most despotic facets of Haitian authoritarian practices (Fatton 2013; Pierre-Charles 1973; Trouillot 1987).

Trouillot argued that the Duvalierist regimes' use of violence appeared to be limitless, total, omnipresent and irrational (1990, 169). It was deployed indiscriminately against everyone, irrespective of position, group or politics. Gérard Pierre-Charles, an eminent Haitian intellectual and politician, in his book *Radiographie d'Une Dictature* (Radiography of a Dictatorship), characterized the violence deployed by both of the Duvaliers as unlimited and unique in the country's history (1973, 46).

The second characteristic of Duvalierist rule was incompetence. Trouillot (1990) described the Duvalierist regime as "the reign of incompetency, where all power lay with mediocre individuals" (173). Indeed, because of the extreme violence imposed by the Duvaliers, many educated Haitians were forced to leave the country. It was a political strategy to govern with only the inept individuals in order to ensure loyalty as well as to distribute patronage. Incompetent bureaucrats tend to lean more toward loyalty and faithfulness to those in power. The effect of this form of governing is inefficiency (Hintzen 1998).

Perhaps people accommodated themselves to the violence and incompetence through compliance (Mbembe 2000), as the regime created deep-seated mistrust and fear within Haiti's population. Agents of the regime were located everywhere and were employed to report any hint of disloyalty and opposition, even from their superiors.

The final characteristic that Trouillot described as a condition of power under Duvalier and his son is corruption. Under the Duvalierist state, corruption reached an unprecedented level. It became rife as a practice that spanned from the president to low-ranking public officials. Jean Claude Duvalier, for example, was known for his lavish lifestyle; his wedding to a mulatto member of the Haitian elite, Michèle Bennett, in 1980 was estimated to have cost $3 million (*Haiti Observer* 2013). In the final three years before his oust from power, documents from Haiti's Central Bank showed that he had embezzled more than US$120 million from the government. As a political tactic, the Duvaliers put into place a system of clientelism that exchanged favour and office for loyalty. This provided extended opportunities for embezzlement as the regime's supporters were able to enrich themselves in exchange for their loyalty. Trouillot wrote:

> Corruption became the very foundation of the administrative machine, its raison d'être. One entered the state apparatus only to benefit from it, for there was no pretence about doing anything else. Corruption became politically effective as never before; it guaranteed the unconditional endorsement of the regime's supporters. (1990, 176)

The peasantry was particularly victim to the Duvalier regime, notwithstanding their almost absolute support that propelled Francois Duvalier's rise to power. They were not exempt from his cruelty and brutality, and they suffered mainly from the inefficiency of the regime. The Duvaliers failed to improve the peasantry's material conditions and denied them access to political rights (Fatton 2013). The survival of the regime came to be "more easily maintained through extreme centralization" than through the projects that benefited the rural peasantry in which negligible investments were made (Trouillot 1990, 176). The peasants remained illiterate, poor and neglected by the state. They continued to be treated as *moun andeyo* (outside people), without the full rights of Haitian citizens (Fatton 2013). In this manner, civil society was totally excluded from the political process. Forces of the nation were mobilized to ensure regime survival and guarantee that the interests of the state were realized. To ensure regime survival, a paramilitary force called the *Tonton Macoutes* was organized as a militia to terrorize the population and maintain compliance.

My argument thus far is that violence, incompetence and corruption were rampant under the Duvalier regime. Their effects on the nation were destructive, consistent with the conditions for regime survival employed in most Caribbean and Latin American countries, as described by Hintzen (1998, 2018). They foreclosed any possibility for the national government to implement the conditions necessary for development and economic progress.

The Duvalierist regimes maintained order in the country, but at a high cost, the cost of survival, through a reinforcing of an ideology, patronage, effective measures of control, coercion and international realignment. The two Duvalier regimes also came to depend on relations with the United States in their strategy for survival. They were able to remain in power for almost thirty years. In this regard, the regime of the two Duvaliers resembled that of the American occupation, which was also embedded in forms of control and coercion supported by a foreign military force.

The fall of Jean Claude Duvalier came about because of a rupture in the conditions that guaranteed the regimes' survival – a complete break with the ideology of *noirism* that mainly held Papa Doc in power and that advocated for the rehabilitation of the Black middle class and the creation of a Black bourgeoisie. Through such ideology, the state under Papa Doc was able to mobilize the symbolic power of its identification with the Black Creole-speaking nation and to speak on their behalf. When Jean Claude Duvalier came to power in 1971, he undermined the symbolic capital of his father by aligning with the coloured elite through his marriage with Michèle Bennett, a mulatto woman. The power of the *noirisme* ideology began to fade away, and the state was no longer able to maintain its narrative as representative of the nation. As a result, the regime lost its ability to discipline, regulate, co-opt and control the population, leading to its loss of power. The fall of Duvalier did not, however, change the material or political conditions in the country. Instead, since 1986, Haiti has sunk more deeply into political instability.

There have always been periods, however, where coercion, control, co-optation and surveillance fail and where mobilization of the nation begins to challenge state interests. These were the circumstances that brought Duvalier to power. It was also the condition that brought a radical Roman Catholic priest named Jean Bertrand Aristide to power with the popular support of the "nation" pitted against the state and its international allies. Aristide was elected to power because of his *Lavalas* movement. *Lavalas* is the Creole word for avalanche. The *Lavalas* is a movement that promised a sweeping eradication of social and economic inequalities and the resurrection of the popular masses. The movement articulated rhetoric against both national and international elites and rendered them responsible for the misery and poverty of the masses. The state effects of national and global forces undermined the movement. Those forces overthrew Aristide through a coup d'état on 29 September 1991. Because of intense popular mobilizations both nationally and internationally, Aristide was brought to power after three years in exile but only under the conditions of the application of neoliberal policy, which compromised the nature of the *Lavalas* movement and Aristide's government's policies.

There has always been tension between the governing apparatus of the state and the people. Antonio Gramsci analysed how this tension is generally managed in his theorization of hegemony. This term refers to the ways in which a ruling class gains consent to rule from those it subjugates (Eagleton 1991). Analysing the capitalist state, Gramsci identified two spheres that constitute the capitalist state: a political society and a civil society. The latter refers to the public sphere, where ideas and beliefs are shaped, reproduced and legitimized (Heywood 1994). Legitimacy here is gained through consent rather than force. Consent is manufactured through the control of the superstructure, which includes education, religion and cultural norms.

A counter-hegemony that challenges the power of the ruling group can emerge from civil society, which contests the dominant class's rules, norms, ideas and legitimacy and articulates novel visions and ideas for the transformation of society. Political crises that challenge the ruling group are produced out of a crisis of hegemony itself. This can occur when the dominant class (the state) fails to articulate a vision of development that includes the subaltern groups (the nation), and conditions for regime survival are no longer effective. These are the conditions that Haiti has been experiencing for a considerable period, especially since 1986.

So far, I have argued that the Haitian popular class, organized into the nation, has been engaged in a continuous struggle against the state's governing apparatus. This struggle intensified between 1986 and 2010. The administrations that succeeded Jean Claude Duvalier, with the exception of Jean Bertrand Aristide, failed to articulate a clear or coherent ideology. Meanwhile, the topography of global politics began to erode the conditions of control and coercion that facilitated the Duvalier regimes' survival. The result has been constant political instability in the country.

Political violence and instability have been a pervasive feature of Haitian politics since Haiti's independence. Throughout the nineteenth century and before the period of American occupation, most of Haiti's presidents gained power through *coup d'état*[2] or following a triumphant insurrection (Pierre-Charles 1973). Since 1986, the country has witnessed a resurgence of recurring political crises, violence and rapid governmental changes – similar to what the country experienced before the American occupation when five presidents gained and lost power. Between 1986 and 2010, Haiti saw more than twenty different governments[3] come to power, each serving an average tenure of just over a year (see table 4.1). This frequent turnover underscores the political instability that characterized the country during this period. Between 1986 and 2010, René Préval was the only president to have completed his term of office and to have completed a second term. He remained in power even under conditions of deteriorating economic performance and his capitulation to neoliberalism. His success can be explained by his ability to build on the ideology of *Lavalas* that appealed directly to the subaltern nation, his skilful use of patronage for political support, his ability to develop clientelistic ties with the economic elites and a repositioning of his international alignment. The latter is an essential condition for regime survival, as we have seen with Hintzen (1998, 2018). Particularly during his second term, René Préval generated opposition support and silence through the distribution of political positions and jobs. He also used the resources of the state to distribute patronage to the elites through lucrative contracts.

Table 4.1: Haiti's Governments, 1986–2016[4]

Number	Governments/ Administration	Period Served	Time Served
1	President: Henri Namphy (Military junta)	02/1986 to 02/1988	2 years
2	President: Leslie F. Manigat	02/1988 to 06/1988	4 months
3	President: Henri Namphy (Military government)	06/1988 to 09/1988	3 months
4	President Prosper Avril (Military government)	09/1988 to 03/1990	20 months
5	Acting President: Hérard Abraham (Military government)	03/1990 to 03/1990	3 days
6	President: Ertha Pascal-Trouillot	03/1990 to 02/1991	10 months
7	President: Jean-Bertrand Aristide Prime Minister: René Préval	02/1991 to 09/1991 and 10/1994 to 0/1996	7 months in Haiti (2 years in exile)

Table 4.1: Haiti's Governments, 1986–2016 (contd)

Number	Governments/ Administration	Period Served	Time Served
8	President: Joseph C. Nerette	10/1991 to 06/1992	7 months
	Prime Minister: Jean-Jacques Honorat	10/1991 to 06/1992	7 months
9	No president		
	Prime Minister: Marc Bazin	06/1992 to 06/1993	12 months
10	President: Emile Jonassaint	06/1993 to 10/1994	4 months
	No Prime Minister		
11	President: Jean-Bertand Aristide	10/1994 to 02/1996	16 months
	Prime Ministers:	11/1994 to 10/1995	11 months
	Smark Michel	10/1995 to 02/1996	5 months
	Claudette Werleigh		
12	President: René Préval	02/1996 to 02/2001	5 years
	Prime Ministers:		
	Rosny Smart	05/1996 to 06/1997	14 months
	Jacques Edouard Alexis	03/1999 to 02/2001	23 months
	No Prime Minister since	06/1997 to 03/1999	–
13	President: Jean Bertrand Aristide	02/2001 to 02/2004	3 years
	Prime Ministers:	02/2001 to 01/2002	11 months
	Jean Marie Chérestal	03/2002 to 02/2004	23 months
	Yvon Neptune		
14	President: Boniface Alexandre	02/2004 to 05/2006	27 months
	Prime Minister: Gerard Latortue	03/2004 to 06/2006	27 months
15	President: René Préval	05/2006 to 05/2011	5 years
	Prime Ministers:		
	Jacques Edouard Alexis	06/2006 to 04/2008	22 months
	Michelle Pierre Louis	09/2008 to 11/2009	14 months
	Jean-Max Bellerive	11/2009 to 10/2011	23 months

These rapid changes in government point to the instability produced by the fracture between the state and nation, with the latter now incorporating the urban migrants from the peasantry as an underclass. Trouillot's peasantry in today's Haiti has collapsed over the last four decades. The new divide is produced out of a disjuncture between what Robert Fatton (2007) calls the "possessing class" and subaltern groups. The rapid changes in government are produced out of such a disjuncture and the inability of the elite to maintain control of the state and its resources. Such a disjuncture articulates the limits of the Haitian state as an instrument of genuine development and a means of creating the conditions for effective democracy (Hintzen 2018).

The Haitian state has become a predatory state (Dupuy 1997, 2005; Fatton 2002; Maguire 2008; Mehan 2004). Predation, in this way, has become a condition for holding power. Similar observations have also been made in West Indian states in the region. In his article, "Towards a New Democracy in the Caribbean: Local Empowerment and the New Global Order", Percy Hintzen (2018) argues that depriving the subalterns of access to effective participation in governance and economic processes has allowed the middle class and upper strata to use illegal means and pervasive practices of corruption in order to gain and maintain state control. In turn, the masses respond to such conditions by developing their own political practices and social and economic agencies. Hintzen (2018) writes:

> The lower strata, as the overwhelming majority, by and large, are without these opportunities, except indirectly through forms of patronage and clientelism. They are forced to create their own conditions for economic opportunity, their own extrajudicial forms of political practice (including riots), and their own forms of social welfare and protective security. For them, the 'societal arrangements', formed and fashioned to satisfy social needs through the guarantee of economic and political rights occur outside governing practice. (98)

The way state power has been gained, constituted and maintained encapsulates the structural and historical conditions that produce precarity within the masses, the majority of the population. It also produces the profound vulnerabilities that we noticed on 12 January 2010.

Haiti Before the 2010 Earthquake: Weak Economy, Structural Poverty and Vulnerable Population

There have been profound vulnerabilities in Haiti that have produced forms of extreme precarity prior to the earthquake. During the two decades preceding the earthquake, Haiti's economic growth had been declining, while poverty and income inequality were rising (World Bank 2007, 2015). During the 1990s and 2000s, the average GDP growth was below 1 per cent, which was much lower than the 3.5 per cent average growth of Latin American Countries (Singh and Barton-Dock 2015, 43). The country experienced some short-lived positive growth in the years following 1994 when President Aristide was ousted from power after seven months in office. The United States reinstated him after agreeing to the neoliberal agenda. The initial growth was immediately followed by five subsequent years of negative growth (Singh and Barton-Dock 2015, 43) that continued to contribute to massive urban migration and susceptibility to natural disasters (table 4.2) under conditions of dramatically increased vulnerability for the population.

The country maintained its position in the low human development category in UNDP's Human Development rankings. Out of 189 countries and territories, Haiti was positioned at 168 in these rankings (UNDP 2019). Particularly during the two years before the earthquake, the social and economic conditions in Haiti were worsening. More than 3.3 million Haitians were threatened by food insecurity, which caused food riots to erupt in diverse regions of the country (International Crisis Group 2009). The worsening of the economic situation was partly due to four tropical storms and hurricanes that hit the country during August and September of 2008 (International Crisis Group 2009; Singh and Barton-Dock 2015). Eight hundred people were killed, one million were affected, and widespread damage affected the country's already minimal infrastructure, which exacerbated the food shortage (ALNAP 2010; International Crisis Group 2009; Rencoret 2010).[5]

Table 4.2: Summary of the Last Three Disasters in Haiti Before the 2010 Earthquake[6]

Year	Events	Effect on GDP	Individuals Affected	Dead
2004	Hurricane Jeanne	7% of GDP	300,000	5,000
2007	Hurricanes Dean and Noel	2% of GDP	194,000	330
2008	Hurricanes Fay, Gustav, Hanna, and Ike	15% of GDP	1,000,000	800
Total	N/A	24% of GDP	1,494,000	6,130

Source: Republic of Haiti, Post-Disaster Needs Assessment (PDNA) 2010

In 2008, the economy grew only slightly by 1.3 per cent against an inflation rate of 13 per cent, resulting in a negative real growth rate. During the same year, nearly three-quarters of the population was living below $2 a day (International Crisis Group 2009; World Bank 2009a). In 2009, 50.6 per cent of the population was living in urban areas, but 83 per cent of them resided in high-density slums with significant health concerns. Only 30 per cent of the population had access to some form of health care, while 70 per cent of the population had no access to health care at all (ALNAP 2010). There was also a reduction in remittances during the period as a result of the global recession and the economic crisis in the United States. This rendered the conditions even more dire and precarious. Transfers to Haiti from remittances dropped by 15 per cent (Haiti Libre 2013). It was in the face of these deplorable social and economic conditions and profound vulnerability that the earthquake hit Haiti on 12 January 2010.

Summary

This chapter relies significantly on both Hintzen's scholarship regarding the Costs of Regime Survival and Trouillot's *Haiti: State Against Nation* to explore the conditions under which state power is acquired, constituted and perpetuated in Haiti – conditions that encompass control, coercion and violence. Although these conditions are not exclusive to Haiti, I have demonstrated that they have played a crucial and determining role in the country since its independence and have intensified since 1986. I have argued that the manner in which state power has been established and its consequences have generated the historical contexts that engender precarity among the vast majority of the Haitian population, the subaltern.

I also argued that there have been instances when strategies for regime survival have become ineffective and when regimentation, regulation, control, surveillance, and coercion have ceased to function; this was what precipitated the fall of Duvalier. When such conditions arise, opportunities present themselves for a new kind of discourse. These can offer possibilities for the emergence of novel strategies capable of altering the conditions that create precarity in the first place, leading to genuine economic development and supporting democracy. Such conditions failed to emerge and take root following the fall of the Duvalierist regime. Instead, the state continues to undermine the nation. The dominant class and political elites remain beneficiaries of the system to the detriment of the poor. The calamities experienced by the country on 12 January 2010 only reflect the extent to which the profound disjuncture between the state and the nation has rendered Haitian governments ineffective and the degree to which Haiti's vulnerability to disaster has increased due to the manner in which state power is constituted.

FIVE

Disjunctures: Between Hope and Reality

It is our collective responsibility as a Nation – nonprofit organizations and the public and private sectors – to implement effective standards and codes that sustain safe and resilient structures.

President Barack Obama

Immediately following the earthquake, the international community mobilized a massive support effort to help the devastated country. Individuals around the world, Haitians in the diaspora, international governments, UN agencies and NGOs were all involved in the effort. There was an enormous influx of NGOs, adding to the thousands that were already in the country before the earthquake. Many came from the United States, perhaps because of the history of US-based NGO presence in the country, as well as its bilateral funding, notably from USAID. The Haitian government was clearly overwhelmed. Its ability to cope was made even more difficult in the wake of the loss of essential government personnel. No government ministers died, but numerous human losses occurred in the administrative apparatus. Many public servants spent the first few days after the earthquake trying to locate and care for their loved ones (Grünewald and Renaudin 2010).

Material damages in the public administration were also enormous. According to the Haitian government, thirteen of fifteen government ministry buildings collapsed, and the majority of the public administration buildings, including the Presidential Palace, the

Parliament and the Palace of Justice (GOH 2010), were completely or partially destroyed. These conditions, in addition to grave damage to the country's transportation, communication and energy infrastructure, greatly limited the capacity of the administration, thus hindering the government's ability to manage the crisis.

Even before the disaster, the government exercised very limited control over the NGOs. Generally, NGOs benefit from relative autonomy and freedom from state jurisdiction. In Haiti, their autonomy had been even greater due to the ineffectiveness of the state. The damage that the government suffered as a result of the earthquake automatically lessened the government's capacity to coordinate the NGOs and aid agencies in the disaster relief efforts.

Figure 5.1: Haiti's National Palace Before the Earthquake[1]
Source: Getty Images

In the face of government incapacity and ineffectiveness, the UN's Office for the Coordination of Humanitarian Affairs (OCHA) began to coordinate relief efforts. Thus, assessments of damage and the need for material and financial assistance fell to the Humanitarian Country Team (HCT). The HCT was already present and operating in the country following the tropical storms and hurricanes that struck the country in August and September 2008. Those events killed more than eight hundred Haitians, affected nearly one million, and exacerbated food shortages and poverty in Haiti (International Crisis Group 2009).

Within three days of the earthquake, Haiti made its first request for money based on a rapid remote-sensing assessment of the damage. The first request for US$575 million was made on 15 January 2010. About a month later, the request was increased to US$1.4 billion. This would support the need for a full humanitarian intervention and for resources to cover the activities of seventy-six aid organizations operative in the country (Rencoret et al. 2010). This amounted to the largest-ever natural disaster request for Haiti (Rencoret et al. 2010, 23).

By 30 April, an estimated 47–55 per cent of the revised US$1.4 billion request was already disbursed (Rencoret et al. 2010). In the wake of the disaster, some countries and funding agencies, including G7's members (Canada, United States, UK, France, Germany, Italy and Japan), the Inter-American Development Bank and Venezuela agreed to forgive Haiti's outstanding debt. Haiti's Caribbean neighbours also mobilized disaster aid, particularly through the Caribbean Catastrophic Risk Insurance Facility (CCRIF), which gave a payout totalling US$7.75 million in disaster assistance directly to the Haitian government (Rencoret et al. 2010).

Until that time, the Haitian government was critically involved in the process. It engaged in systematic efforts to get relief funding, secure funding commitments and produce an Action Plan for National Recovery and Development. In this regard, a series of outreach meetings with key constituencies were held in preparation for a planned donor conference to seek feedback on and support for the government's strategic plan. The meetings were as follows (UN 2010):

- 15 March: Consultation with citizens in Haiti through focus group discussions called "Voice of the Voiceless" consultations. (The Office of the Special Envoy and the United Nations in Haiti led this effort.)

- 15 March: Consultation with Haitian and international private sector representatives hosted by the Inter-American Development Bank in Port-au-Prince.

- 23 March: Consultation with Haitian Diaspora hosted by the Organization of American States in Washington, DC.

- 23 March: Consultation with local government authorities hosted by France in Saint Martin.

- 25 March: The Office of the Special Envoy, Interaction, and the European Union hosted a consultation with NGOs in New York. NGOs from Haiti, the Americas and Europe participated.

The International Donors' Conference

The most significant funding commitment was coordinated by the UN at the International Donors' Conference, *Toward a New Future for Haiti*, held in New York on 31 March. There was an important international representation of delegates at the conference. The photograph below signifies the degree of seriousness the international community was bringing to the disaster by the presence of some of the world's most important figures.

Figure 5.2:   International Donors' Conference, Toward a New Future for Haiti
Source: Getty Images

From left to right sat US Secretary of State Hillary Clinton, UN Secretary-General Ban Ki-moon, Haitian President Rene G. Préval, and former US President Bill J. Clinton. There were also many other important world leaders present at the conference. For example, Robert Zoellick, president of the World Bank; Luis Alberto Moreno, president of the Inter-American Bank of Development; Campton Bourne, representing the Caribbean Development Bank; Percival James Paterson, former prime minister of Jamaica, representing CARICOM; other world leaders such as Bernard Kouchener, Minister for Foreign Affairs in France; Gerald Tremblay, the mayor of Montreal; Antonio Simoes, Brazil Undersecretary for South America and the Caribbean, and representatives of important civil society organizations (C-SPAN 2010).

There was a sense of optimism and hope for Haiti that inspired every Haitian on the eve of the International Donor's Conference in New York titled "Toward a New Future for Haiti" (full speech in the Appendix), which was set to be held on Wednesday, 31 March 2010. It was believed that the earthquake created a unique opportunity for Haiti to rise from poverty and create a better life for its people. René Préval, the Haitian president at that time, called the conference a "rendezvous with history", "a pact to build a new Haiti", and a "Haiti transformed". He declared, "I am confident that, together, we can set Haiti on the road to a new and very different future… And for Haiti, hope begins this Wednesday in New York".

Several important remarks were made at the conference on Wednesday, 31 March 2010. The president of Haiti, René Préval, shared his hope to rebuild a new Haiti. Jean-Max Bellerive, Haiti's prime minister, presented the Haitian Government Action Plan to rebuild the country, a plan that he said, "has been formed through a broad-based consultation with the private sector, Non-Governmental Organizations, the Haitian diaspora and the international community" (UN 2010). However, it is important here to examine and discuss the opening statement[2] of the UN secretary general, Ban Ki-moon, and the remarks[3] of US Secretary of State, Hillary Clinton.

In his address, Ban Ki-moon argued and advocated for the incorporation of sustainable development goals in the rebuilding process.

He declared, "Our goal is not just to rebuild. It is to build back better." He advocated for a new Haiti, a developed Haiti, "where the majority of people no longer live in deep poverty, where they can go to school and enjoy better health, where they have better options than going without jobs or leaving the country altogether". He also announced during the conference the creation of the Interim Haiti Recovery Commission, which would oversee the implementation of the Government of Haiti's Action Plan for National Recovery and Development. The commission would also "ensure that the international assistance is aligned with the priorities of the Haitian People and their government, ensuring accountability and transparency" (OSGSA 2010). The commission was co-chaired by Haiti's Prime Minister Jean Max Bellerive and the former president of the United States, Bill Clinton.

The US secretary of state, Hillary Clinton also advocated for sustainable development (full speech in the Appendix). In her statement, she addressed the issues of Haitian migration. She underscored the international humanitarian commitment to Haiti's future, stressing the importance of safe housing, sustainable economic growth, robust health and education systems and accountable institutions. She argued that if Haiti realizes a "broad-based, sustainable economic growth, it can create opportunity across the country", then there would be no need for Haitians to migrate from rural areas to Port-au-Prince or leave the country. She also highlighted the problems of hunger, environmental degradation, weakness of the state and the necessity for the international community to do things differently and provide relief in ways that could produce positive results for the people of Haiti. She warned of the consequences of insufficient or poorly coordinated rebuilding efforts, urging a coordinated, transparent approach from both Haitian leaders and the global community. She argued that the conference was intended to promote effective aid delivery and long-term investment in Haiti's recovery. She highlighted two possible futures for the country: one in which international support facilitates rebuilding, leading to stability, economic growth and improved infrastructure; and another defined by ongoing hardship, including migration, food insecurity, and political instability, should aid efforts fall short or be mismanaged. She called for Haiti's leaders to take responsibility for reconstruction, urged global cooperation in effective aid delivery and stressed the importance of sustained commitment and accountability from all stakeholders to achieve lasting positive change for Haiti. Both Hillary Clinton and Ban Ki-moon, therefore, advocated for disaster relief aid to be guided by principles of sustainable development, effective and responsible governance and the promotion of long-term resilience.

Ban Ki-moon also praised former President Préval and Haiti's then-prime minister, Jean-Max Bellerive, for their comprehensive national strategic plan to guide Haiti's recovery and reconstruction. He argued that the plan emphasizes not just rebuilding but "building back better", aiming for a new Haiti where poverty is reduced, education and health care are improved, and economic opportunities are created to prevent migration. He announced that the Interim Haiti Recovery Commission is proposed to oversee $3.9 billion in funding over eighteen months, with a total reconstruction estimate of $11.5 billion over the next decade. As reconstruction was ongoing, they would continue to provide emergency relief, food, sanitation, health care and, most urgently at that moment, shelter.

Donors pledged US$9.9 billion of funding for the reconstruction and recovery of Haiti. Of this, US$5.3 billion was to be disbursed over two years in support of the Action Plan for National Recovery and Development Plan that the Haitian government designed following the earthquake, based on the results of the Post-Disaster Needs Assessment (Rencoret et al. 2010). In the two years following the earthquake, Haiti received US$6.43 billion.

However, most of this money was not disbursed to the government directly but channelled to the INGOs, NGOs and other relief agencies.

Notwithstanding the firm commitments to sustainable development and good governance expressed at the conference, these were not incorporated into disaster relief efforts. Ten years after the earthquake, this failure manifested itself as a failure in recovery efforts. This failure was evidenced in the responses to a survey I conducted to assess the effectiveness of the recovery effort and whether resilience was incorporated into it. I discuss the results of the survey in the next section of this chapter.

The Resilience Survey: Findings and Analysis

The objective of the survey was to determine whether respondents achieved the goals of resilience through self-assessments of recovery. The survey was conducted in three communes in Port-au-Prince. Port-au-Prince is a large metropolitan area constituted by eight communes: Port-au-Prince (the downtown area, which shares the name with the greater city), Carrefour, Gressier, Cité Soleil, Delmas, Tabarre, Pétion Ville and Kenscoff. The sample survey was administered to 889 households.

The three surveys were conducted in the communes of Port-au-Prince, Delmas and the suburb of Carrefour (see table 5.1). These three communes were chosen to represent the greater Port-au-Prince area. Delmas is located on the northern side of Port-au-Prince, the commune of Port-au-Prince is in the centre and Carrefour is on the south side of Port-au-Prince. The earthquake severely damaged these three communes. Although they are part of the greater Port-au-Prince area, they share some socio-economic characteristics that are important to highlight here.

Figure 5.3:   Map of Haiti. Port-au-Prince Indicated with a Red Star
Source: Getty Images

Demography and Social-Economic Status

Table 5.1 below presents the economic and demographic data across the three communes.

Table 5.1: Sample Description by Commune

	Average	Delmas	Commune Port-au-Prince	Carrefour
Sample size (persons)	889 (total)	329	288	272
Household size (persons)	4.68	4.85	4.65	4.49
Children in household (%)	29.3	25.2	30.7	32.9
Working in household (%)	33.9	32.5	33.5	36.1
Level of education (%)				
No schooling	5.6	3.7	5.9	7.7
Primary	23.8	17.7	23.1	32.0
High school	48.0	51.5	46.2	45.6
Vocational school	7.8	11.6	8.7	2.2
College or above	14.8	15.5	16.1	12.5
Work status (%)				
Not employed	19.3	26.8	14.0	15.8
Employed in informal jobs	62.0	53.4	64.3	69.9
Employed in formal jobs	18.7	19.8	21.7	14.3
Neighborhood class (%)				
Working class	32.3	13.7	39.2	47.4
Middle class	65.9	84.8	58.0	51.5
Upper class	1.8	1.5	2.8	1.1

Source: 2019 Haiti Resilience Survey (Analytic N=889)

The Commune of Port-au-Prince

The commune of Port-au-Prince is located at the centre of the greater Port-au-Prince area. It is largely characterized by its social and economic diversity. It is the largest commercial centre of Haiti. The majority of government offices are located in the commune.

According to table 5.1, 39 per cent of the population in Port-au-Prince identified as working class, while 58 per cent identified as middle class. Port-au-Prince has the highest number of people self-identified as upper class, which represents 2.8 per cent of its population. It also has the lowest number of unemployed people among the three communes. Only 14 per cent of the residents of the commune are unemployed. However, most people in the commune are working in the informal sector. Almost 22 per cent hold a formal job, which, among the three communes, represents the highest proportion of people formally employed.

Delmas

The commune of Delmas is located in the northern part of the capital. It represents the third most populated commune in Port-au-Prince, and in the whole country. It is the location of many industrial and commercial enterprises. It is the wealthiest community in Haiti based on the tax revenue they collect. Delmas collects more tax revenue than any other commune or suburb in Port-au-Prince.

Delmas is a middle- to high-income community. About 80 per cent of its residents self-reported that they have at least a secondary education, compared to 71 per cent in Port-au-Prince and 60 per cent in Carrefour. About 85 per cent of Delmas residents consider themselves middle class (table 5.1). Less than 14 per cent consider themselves working class. Only 3.7 per cent self-reported as having no education, compared to 5.9 per cent in the commune of Port-au-Prince and 7.7 per cent in the commune of Carrefour.

Delmas also has better infrastructure compared to the rest of the capital. The population has access to clean water and excellent schools. One of the best private hospitals in the country is in Delmas. Many Haitians in the diaspora who are supporting family members in Port-au-Prince often choose Delmas for their parents or family members' residences because of its modern urban infrastructure.

However, Delmas has the highest unemployment rate. Nearly 27 per cent of its residents have reported to be unemployed, compared to 14 per cent in Port-au-Prince and 15.8 per cent in Carrefour. It seems that the commune may have a "high dependency ratio", meaning family members who are dependent on others and therefore are not employed. Those they depend on can include business owners, professionals and people in the diaspora.

Carrefour

Carrefour is located on the south side of the capital. It has the highest number of uneducated people among the three cities. Nearly 40 per cent of the population reported having no secondary education at all, compared to 29 per cent in the commune of Port-au-Prince and 21.4 per cent in Delmas. About one-third of the population has a primary education, nearly 46 per cent have high school diplomas and 12.5 per cent have some kind of college education (table 5.1).

Carrefour is the home of the largest lower-class population among the three cities. Nearly half of the population identifies as working class, while a little more than half identifies as middle class. Carrefour has the lowest number of people that identify themselves as upper class, which represents only 1 per cent of the city's population. About 70 per cent of the Carrefour population earns their living from informal jobs. Only 14.3 per cent of the population is employed in the formal sector.

The Damages and Life Perturbation

This section analyses both the damages and perturbations that the earthquake caused in the lives of the people of Port-au-Prince based on the three communes surveyed. First, we proceed to provide a general assessment of the damages and suffering as a result of the earthquake. Second, we consider the perturbations caused by the earthquake as a result of loss of health, property and income.

Table 5.2: *General Damage Assessment: Distribution of Households by Commune According to Whether They Declared Having Suffered Losses Resulting from the Earthquake*

How do you evaluate the losses resulting from the earthquake of 12 January, 2010? (read the response categories)					
Neighbourhood	No Loss at All (%)	Some Losses (%)	Much Loss (%)	Lost Everything (%)	Total (%)
Delmas	17.2	52.4	21.4	9.0	100.0
Port-au-Prince	10.0	49.0	32.4	8.6	100.0
Carrefour	2.9	59.0	35.2	2.9	100.0
Average	10.5	53.3	29.2	7.0	100.0

Source: Haiti Resilience Survey (Analytic N=889)

Table 5.2 presents the households assessment of damage as a result of the earthquake. We asked the question: How do you evaluate the losses resulting from the earthquake on 12 January 2010? The categories of response were 0=no loss; 1 = some loss; 2=much loss; 3=total loss.

The table demonstrates extensive damages across all the communities. About 83 per cent of households in Delmas experienced some degree of losses, compared to 90 per cent in Port-au-Prince and nearly every household in Carrefour experienced some degree of loss and damages.

While the commune of Delmas had the largest number of households that experienced no loss at all, it also had the highest number of households that lost everything: 9 per cent in Delmas compared to nearly 3 per cent in Carrefour. However, Carrefour has the highest number of respondents reporting that they had many losses: 35.2 per cent. The difference between Delmas and the commune of Port-au-Prince regarding the number of households declared to have lost everything remains very small. Out of all respondents, 8.6 per cent of residents surveyed in the commune of Port-au-Prince reported that they lost everything, compared to the 9 per cent in Delmas. The conclusion is that all the communes had suffered significantly from the earthquake.

Table 5.3: Long-Term Health Perturbances: Distribution of Households by Municipality According to Whether They Declare Having Chronic Health Problems Resulting from the Earthquake

Is there anyone in your household who has long-term health problems as a result of the 2010 earthquake?			
Municipality/ Commune	**No (%)**	**Yes (%)**	**Total (%)**
Delmas	84.6	15.4	100.0
Port-au-Prince	77.2	22.8	100.0
Carrefour	72.9	27.1	100.0
Average	78.7	21.3	100.0

Source: Haiti Resilience Survey (Analytic N=889)

Table 5.3 assesses the long-term health problem across the communes as a result of the consequences of the earthquake. We asked the question:

Is there anyone in your household who has long-term health problems as a result of the 2010 earthquake? The categories of response were: 0 = no; 1 = yes.

The figures demonstrate that the residents in Delmas expressed slightly less long-term health concerns compared to the residents in Port-au-Prince and Carrefour. Although the difference between the residents in Carrefour and those in Port-au-Prince are almost insignificant, the data shows Carrefour suffered slightly more from long-term health issues than the residents of Port-au-Prince. We can conclude that the commune of Carrefour suffered more from long-term health problems compared to the other communes' residents. However, the differences among the three communes were minimal.

Table 5.4: Loss of Property

Did you lose your home during the 2010 earthquake?			
Municipality/ Commune	**No (%)**	**Yes (%)**	**Total (%)**
Delmas	63.3	36.7	100.0
Port-au-Prince	73.4	26.6	100.0
Carrefour	84.2	15.8	100.0
Average	**73.0**	**27.0**	**100.0**

Source: Haiti Resilience Survey (Analytic N=889)

Table 5.4 presents the household assessment of damages resulting from the earthquake across the three communes as it relates to residents indicating having lost their homes. We asked the question: Did you lose your home during the earthquake? The data shows that Delmas was struck hardest by the earthquake with the highest assessed losses of homes. Nearly 37 per cent of households in Delmas declared having lost their homes, compared to 26.7 per cent in Port-au-Prince and 15.8 per cent in Carrefour. The data indicates also that the household assessment of damage was less in Carrefour compared to the two other communes. This can be explained by the fact that the homes in Carrefour were more resilient because of their simplicity.

Table 5.5: Financial Loss: Distribution of Households Having Suffered a Loss of Income Due to the Earthquake

Did you lose your job after the 12 January 2010, earthquake?			
Municipality/ Commune	**No (%)**	**Yes (%)**	**Total (%)**
Delmas	79.2	20.8	100.0
Port-au-Prince	77.2	22.8	100.0
Carrefour	72.5	27.5	100.0
Average	**76.5**	**23.5**	**100.0**

Source: Haiti Resilience Survey (Analytic N=889)

Table 5.5 indicates the household assessment of their financial loss resulting from the earthquake. We asked the question: Did you (or any member of the household) lose your job after the 12 January 2010, earthquake? The categories of response were: 0 = no; 1 = yes. Based on the respondents' assessment, the data indicates a slightly lower number of individuals lost their income in Delmas compared to Port-au-Prince. The individual assessments of income lost was higher in Carrefour. Compared to Delmas, about 7 per cent more respondents in the commune declared having lost their income as a result of the earthquake. This difference between the two communes may be explained by the fact that Delmas has a higher dependency ratio than Carrefour. As a result, fewer people lost their incomes as a result of the earthquake.

Recuperation and Recovery

This section analyses the perceived household recovery from the earthquake. I examine the respondents' assessment as to the extent to which their households have been able to regain the same level of social and economic capacity as before the earthquake. We asked the question: how far have you recovered from the 2010 earthquake? The categories of answer were: 1 = no recuperation at all; 2 = somewhat recuperated; 3 = largely recuperated; 4 = completely recuperated.

Table 5.6: Perceived Recovery: Distribution of Households Affected by the Earthquake by Commune and According to Their Level of Recovery

How far have you recovered from the 2010 earthquake? (read the response modalities)					
Municipality/ City	No Recuperation at All (%)	Somewhat Recuperated (%)	Largely Recuperated (%)	Completely Recuperated (%)	Total (%)
Delmas	17.2	63.3	9.3	10.2	100.0
Port-au-Prince	19.3	63.4	9.7	7.6	100.0
Carrefour	21.6	56.0	14.3	8.1	100.0
Average	**19.2**	**61.1**	**10.9**	**8.7**	**100.0**

Source: Haiti Resilience Survey (Analytic N=889)

The data in table 5.6 shows a consensus in assessments that there has been very little recovery among the households across the three communes. On average, only a few families indicated they were able to recover from the earthquake. More than 90 per cent of households across all three communes self-reported they had not fully recovered from the consequences of the earthquake.

Discussions

There are serious disjunctures between commitments expressed at the conference and what was put into practice: The purpose of the first set of figures was to demonstrate differences in vulnerabilities across the three communes based on the effects of the earthquake. The data shows all the communes were severely damaged by the earthquake. The data also indicates very little difference in the assessed damages among the communities except for income losses that can be explained by differences in dependency ratios.

The second set of figures demonstrates that, despite these differences, none of the communities has recovered. More than 90 per cent of respondents declared themselves to have not recovered. As a result, the data indicates that resilience has not occurred in all three of the communes, indicating a failure of recovery efforts. This indicates a failure of efforts to build capacity for resilience into the relief efforts. Two main conclusions can be drawn.

Absence of Culture of Safety and Prevention

Multiple factors can increase a population's vulnerability to disasters. An important factor is the exposure to natural hazards. Exposure to earthquakes, hurricanes, floods or volcanic activity may automatically create vulnerabilities to those events. Florida residents, for example, expect a possible occurrence of hurricanes every year due to the geographical location of the state, which stretches along the Gulf of Mexico. This is the same reality for Caribbean countries like Haiti, Cuba, Jamaica, Puerto Rico and others that experience storms or hurricanes almost regularly. Similarly, countries like Japan, Turkey and Nepal are at risk of earthquakes because of their exposure to fault lines.

A more important factor relates to the way societies handle risks, encourage disaster preparedness and cultivate a culture focused on safety and prevention. Disasters can be less damaging when a society develops a culture of safety and prevention. This idea is reinforced in the UN's Report on the Hyogo World Conference on Disaster Risk Reduction which encourages using knowledge, innovation and education to build a culture of safety and resilience at all levels. The report argues that "disasters can be substantially reduced if people are well informed and motivated towards a culture of disaster prevention and resilience, which in turn requires the collection, compilation, and dissemination of relevant knowledge and information on hazards, vulnerabilities, and capacities" (UN report, note 79, 14). Promoting a culture of safety is not the exclusivity of developed countries. Developing countries can also promote a culture of safety. For example, Cuba has been very successful in its disaster management process and its capacity to promote safety and disaster prevention. As a result, human casualties tend to be extremely low in Cuba when a disaster occurs.

Yet income can play an important role when it comes to households making decisions about safety and disaster prevention. Higher-income individuals tend to live in safer areas. When they live in disaster-prone areas, they tend to live in safer dwellings that follow building codes. Building according to codes can be costly. As it can be costly, people tend to neglect them in places where the rules are not enforced. When a society or a country neglects safety rules and building codes and fails to promote a culture of disaster prevention, it creates a general condition of vulnerability that can potentially affect the entire society regardless of income and level of education. The excessive damage from the quake reported in tables 5.2 and 5.4 translates to a general condition of vulnerability in Haiti, which testifies to complete neglect of a culture of safety and prevention. The earthquake caused severe damage across the board. It caused nearly the same level of destruction in working-class communities like Carrefour as it did in high-income communities like Delmas.

In developing countries, people generally build their own houses. This practice is less prevalent in the United States where homeowners usually purchase homes that a developer of a licensed company builds. Individuals who build their homes in a country like Haiti often circumvent the building codes that prescribe where people can build and the types of construction that can be erected on specific soils. Public infrastructures do not escape this reality either. Chapter 6 gives an idea of the level of destruction the January 2010 earthquake caused to the public infrastructure and government buildings in Port-au-Prince.

Haiti has building codes, but they are not enforced, one NGO official said. The codes are not enforced because of the ineffectiveness of the state but also because of generalized corruption. The agents that are placed to enforce building codes often accept bribes to omit building permits. Therefore, corruption plays a critical role in undermining the culture of safety and prevention in Haiti, which in return tremendously increases people's vulnerability to natural hazards.

The Failure of the NGOs-led Post-disaster Aid

The sense of optimism and hope for a better Haiti has not been concretized in the reality of the Haitian people. What the survey demonstrates is a complete disjuncture between the ambitious goals of the disaster aid discourse articulated through the donors' conference and the real impacts of the aid on the ground. The results of the survey expose both the destructive impact of the quake and the failure of the

NGO intervention in Haiti. On average, 27 per cent of the population in Greater Port-au-Prince lost their home during the quake, nearly 25 per cent of the population lost their livelihoods and 90 per cent of the population suffered some kind of loss because of the quake. Despite the billions of dollars in disaster aid being channelled to Haiti for the recovery and reconstruction of the country, eight years after the earthquake, more than 90 per cent of the population have reported not having recovered from the earthquake. They have not regained the same economic and social conditions they had before the earthquake. This is a massive failure of the NGO post-disaster intervention in Haiti, which I call the catastrophe of disaster aid. The explanation rests fundamentally in the fact that the aid was not delivered in ways that can produce development.

This book is based on Anderson and Woodrow's (1999) approach, which articulates development as the process by which capacities are increased and vulnerabilities decreased. Development can be achieved when people have access to employment, healthcare, education and other entitlements that can raise their capabilities and increase their freedoms. When NGO interventions, specifically in the wake of a disaster, are not geared towards those long-term outcomes, the result can be as catastrophic as the disaster.

For NGO aid to achieve development, two things must be done:

1. The aid must be delivered in ways that can address the root causes of people's vulnerabilities in the first place. In the case of the Haitian population, the root causes of their vulnerability primarily correlate with their conditions of poverty, employment, lack of infrastructure and access to critical public services such as health care. Attacking the root of their vulnerabilities requires considering the profile of the population, their real needs and the set of activities around which they build their livelihood. To that end, NGO projects cannot be designed for the beneficiaries, but with the beneficiaries.

2. NGOs' interventions must be structural, not punctual. Punctual interventions constitute short actions that expect temporary responses to a problem, while structural interventions on the other hand, whether short or long-term, intend to attack

deeper issues and bring long-term solutions. For example, in the face of a population that is experiencing famine, an NGO may decide to bring food for six months to address the existing famine. A structural approach would address the complexity of the underlying social and economic conditions that cause the famine to bring a sustainable solution to the problem.

A more targeted example in the case of Haiti is a project called Cash for Work that was implemented by some NGOs in different communities in Port-au-Prince. The NGOs hire temporary workers for sanitation jobs, such as sewer cleaning. The sewers are often clogged because they cannot respond to the demographic pressure of the communities. Those jobs often last only a few days. When the sewers are clogged again, the NGO may decide, based on their priorities, to implement a new round of cash for work. While cash may produce some temporary economic relief for the beneficiary, it does not address a structural issue which is the lack of employment and sustainable livelihood activities. A better practice would be for the NGOs to build a new drainage system and improve existing infrastructure. This approach will create real jobs that could have long-lasting positive impacts on the local economy. It would stimulate the local economy by creating demand for steel, cement and construction materials, leading to the growth of related industries, boosting local business and creating demand for other goods and services.

Summary

This chapter demonstrated both the degree of concern as well as the extent of the international community's commitment to help Haiti in the wake of the devastating earthquake. This concern led to the International Donors' Conference, "Toward a New Future for Haiti", in which the international community committed to fund a massive relief effort to help the country. The commitments came with the prospect of rebuilding the country through sustainable development projects and goals, reinforcing government effectiveness and promoting disaster resilience. I demonstrated in this chapter that the commitments expressed at the conference were not realized, based on the assessments of respondents.

Nearly $10 billion in disaster aid was channelled to NGOs, but the vast majority of the population has not recovered from the impact of the earthquake. People are claiming that they are still suffering from the effects of the earthquake on their health and economic conditions, which also indicates the failure of resilience, which I will discuss more in the next chapter.

SIX

Rethinking NGOs and Disaster Aid

Never doubt that a small group of thoughtful, committed citizens can
change the world; indeed, it's the only thing that ever has.

Margaret Mead

In chapter 5, I examined the shortcomings of the post-disaster
intervention, attributing its failure primarily to inadequate efforts to
build people's capacities and reduce their vulnerability. Additionally, the
state's incapacity hindered both effective oversight of the intervention
and the development of a dynamic partnership between NGOs and the
government. At this juncture, the question to be answered pertains to
the way disaster aid can be delivered to produce positive outcomes. This
chapter argues for a need to shift funding for disaster aid. Funds should
be distributed to local NGOs and development agencies and coordinated
with effective local governments. The latter can work as collaborators in
the face of an ineffective national government.

Ideally, the national government should be responsible for creating
conditions for development, developing policies and practices that can
build resilience and orienting aid and assistance in a direction that can
create long-term positive outcomes. NGOs cannot replace the state at that
level. Given the national government's incapacities and incapabilities,
the most effective option is for NGOs to implement development work
with local governments and organizations.

Functional Limit of NGO Intervention in Haiti

Regardless of whether the NGOs' intentions are good, dependence on them has severe limitations. Ideally, an effective state is needed to enact sustainable interventions. These limits are echoed in the statements of the university professors I interviewed. Professor Pierre Buteau (Personal Communication 2018) argued that Haiti's development cannot be entrusted to NGOs.

> We saw the intervention of NGOs after the earthquake. These NGOs, in many respects, are solid, honest and serious. They have brought short-term relief, which has improved the situation of people. They have enabled a good number of families to get by. NGOs are very helpful. But we cannot entrust the destiny of a country like Haiti to NGOs with regard to major infrastructure projects, major infrastructure works, also with regard to serious development projects.[1]

Professor Abnel Desamours said that NGOs understand that development is not their responsibility (Interview 2018).

> The responsibility [of development] is not NGOs'. In general, NGO leaders tell you that this is not their mission. They tell you that this is the mission of the state. They tell you that an NGO is not the one to fund long-term activities. First, the very structure of NGOs does not allow them to fund such activities. Sometimes, an NGO exists to solve a problem. The NGO disappears with the resolution of the problem. You can channel the funds through NGOs. But there are things that you cannot ask NGOs to do.[2]

Professor Fritz Dorvilier (2018) posed the problem of the weakness of national institutions and the way aid has been operationalized on the ground:

> Internally, there is the problem of *de-structuration* of internal institutions which has a direct impact on aid effectiveness. If the institutions do not work, if there is a lack of competence in the country, if there is a lack of human resources in the country, if the governance is weak, if the population is at such a low level, aid cannot really work miracles in any way. There is not only the very, very, very high level of poverty, there is also the failure of basic institutions. Internal actors cannot think of aid and operationalize aid on the ground because the needs are so immense; aid is like a drop in the ocean. It is not aid per se; aid is sometimes channelling in areas that should not be used, but

I believe that aid is important. NGOs are important. God only knows! If there were no NGOs in the country, there would be famine, riots, uprisings, etc. Therefore, there is a need for a new approach.

Reinforcing Local NGOs and the Collaboration with Local Governments

Earlier in this book, I discussed the classification of NGOs and the different roles each category of NGO plays based on its mission and the field of intervention. Those roles include agenda setting, relief and social and economic development. Yet NGOs can also be categorized into international and local NGOs, regardless of their field of intervention. International NGOs are organizations whose headquarters are in a different country. The headquarters primarily decide when and how funding is allocated to a given country, the type of project that needs to be implemented and the duration. Those NGOs have a lot of money, resources and power. Because of that, mainly when operating in the context of a weak state, they tend to circumvent the national government.

In contrast, local NGOs refer to organizations born within the territory of their operation. Compared to international NGOs, local NGOs tend to dispose of fewer resources. Generally, they receive funding through members' contributions, private donations, the government, and international NGOs. Except for those that operate in advocacy, local NGOs support the local governments and municipalities in achieving their goals. When they are well established and structured, they can bring positive outcomes. In the face of an ineffective and corrupt state, I argue for a locally based strategy where donors can work with local NGOs, organizations and agencies with proven track records, as well as effective local governments, to ensure the success of their interventions.

Working with local NGOs offers many advantages. First, it reduces the need for international workers and places the money directly in the hands of those who can implement projects on the ground. NGOs often offer expatriates and international workers living conditions that are similar to what they are used to back in their home country. They offer amenities like air-conditioned offices and accommodations in resort-style homes or hotels with Western-like amenities to attract expatriates and other international aid workers. This is done to make the transition and living conditions more comfortable and familiar for individuals coming from Western countries. Without those conditions, international workers would be less likely to work for NGOs if they were required to give up their lifestyle and forced to live under poor and often unpleasant conditions, as is an unfortunate reality in developing countries.

However, some Haitians express considerable resentment over NGOs' use of expatriates and dependence on foreign resources. The administrator of a small local charity who works in health care education voiced those resentments in this way:

> The money, most of it was spent on getting all kinds of stuff to put over here. They come and stay in expensive hotels, rent expensive cars, and go to expensive beaches and stuff like that; you can see that. It is not in their interest to help Haiti develop.[3]

A second advantage that working with local NGOs and agencies provides is that local organizations are more suited to identify the needs of the population. Such an argument was underscored during the focus group that I conducted with local organizations working in Port-au-Prince.

Focus Groups: Methodology

I employed the focus group to complement the data that I got from the institutional ethnography and in-depth interviews. It is necessary to mention that a focus group, as a qualitative method, whether used alone or in triangulation with other methods of data collection, is relevant for evaluative research, analysis of motivational factors, action research or research and development and to facilitate needs analysis (Van Der Maren 1995, 67). I conducted the group discussions with three community organizations that work in Port-au-Prince – one organization per commune. Two of them were women's organizations.

I selected the organizations with the help of the *Cadre de Liaison Inter-Organisation* (CLIO) or the Inter-Organizations Framework, an association of organizations composed of more than sixty-six Haitian and foreign NGOs. With CLIO's assistance, I contacted an organization that works closely with NGOs. They agreed to participate in the research and shared contacts of other organizations that work in different communes. I then contacted about six of these organizations. Only two of them agreed to participate in the research. So I completed the group discussion with a total of three organizations.

I conducted the group discussions with each organization separately. Each group discussion was composed of five to eight individuals. Most of them were board members. A few of them were regular members. The leader of each organization signed the consent form prior to discussion. The groups gave me authorization to record the interviews and to use the official name of their organization. As such, the organization names that I mention below are not pseudonyms but rather their real and official names.

Focus Group Discussion

During a focus group with the *Organization pour le Développement Social et de l'Encadrement Technique des Artisans d'Haiti* (ODSETAD) (Organization for the Social Development and Technical Support of Haiti's Artisans, *Kri Fanm Haiti* (KRIFAH) (Cry of Haiti's Women) and *Sauve Fanm* (Save the Women), the issue of NGO projects as they relate to the real needs of the population surfaced as well. The members of the group suggested that NGOs work with community organizations to design and implement their projects. As community organizations, they believe that they are closer to the population, and they know precisely the kind of projects that will make a difference in people's lives. This was particularly the position of group members from the women's organizations, who pointed out the pervasive neglect by NGOs of women's issues and their financial, economic and social needs. This forced them to organize and advocate for themselves.

Local governments are more aware of the problems that their communities are facing. It is important that local governments are reinforced, and their capacities are increased. Effective collaboration between local governments, local agencies and NGOs can bring successful results, as they identify the real needs of the population and help accordingly. For example, participants in a focus group for one of the organizations voiced the fact that community organizations know the issues that people in the lower strata of the society are experiencing. The participants advocated for better coordination between NGOs and community organizations:

> When it is an NGO that has the power of money in its hands, if there is no framework between the state and NGOs, between community leaders and NGOs, to sit together, identify the needs of the community, we will not find a solution. As long as we don't do this, problems will continue to be repeated every day. Because what is important? When a donor gives money to an NGO for a specific project, for example, he gives money for agriculture. The NGO must act upon specific areas in agriculture if he really wants to support agriculture. Otherwise, you may see the destruction of agriculture instead of supporting and developing national products. That is what we are facing here. (ODSETAD, focus group 2018)[4]

The participants in the focus groups also advocated for what they saw as the most important needs of the population: social security, job creation, reforestation programmes and loan programmes for the informal sector. They argued that while the NGOs may not be able to implement these programmes, as community organizations, they can, and they know how to make them work.

Those arguments helped me to understand the importance of a locally centred intervention as the best way to produce positive outcomes – by directly attacking the roots of people's vulnerabilities and increasing their capacities. It requires local authority guidance and collaboration. More specifically, local NGOs and agencies are more suited for this work. Development NGOs that have the money to intervene can do so as well, but under the guidance of the local community and a framework that is designed by the local governments. One example of such an arrangement is the Morakot post-disaster intervention, which I will discuss more in the next chapter.

Unrealized Goals

In prelude to the International Donors' Conference, the UN secretary-general stated that "our goal is not to rebuild. It is to build back better." He also added, "as we move from emergency aid to longer-term reconstruction, let us recognize that we cannot accept business as usual. What we envision, today, is wholesale national renewal, root to branch

– a sweeping and ambitious exercise in nation-building" (UN 2010). At the conference, promises were made to build a new and sustainable Haiti.

However, ten years later, the goals remain unrealized. For instance, major government buildings have yet to be rebuilt. In fact, most of the structures housing government officials and ministries remain unrepaired or in disrepair, with the Haitian government still operating out of damaged facilities. Perhaps nothing symbolizes the failure of the reconstruction effort more than the still-ruined *Palais National* (National Palace). The Palace was severely damaged during the earthquake and then demolished in 2012. Although Haiti's President Jovenel Moïse announced plans to rebuild the National Palace in 2017 (McFadden 2017), construction has yet to begin. Since the earthquake, the Office of the Presidency has operated out of a temporary structure located in the backyard of the Palace.

Similarly, serving as a reminder of unrealized goals is the *Palais de Justice* (Justice Palace) building, which used to house the *Cour de Cassation* (the equivalent of the Supreme Court in the United States), the Appeal Courts and some other special courts or jurisdictions. The building sustained heavy damage resulting in a partial collapse on 10 January due to the earthquake (see figure 6.1). The structure was still not rebuilt in 2019. The courts are now located in different offices of the capital.

Figure 6.1: ***Palais de Justice* (Justice Palace) after the Earthquake**
Source: iStock Photo

Other important buildings that were destroyed have still not been rebuilt, including the Haitian Parliament. It has not been restored or replaced. According to Haiti Libre (2018), the construction of the new National Parliament was stopped. A new structure with four buildings will be built on the same site as the old parliament.[5] However, I have visited the construction site, and there was no indication that work is ongoing.

Figure 6.2:   *Palais de Justice* (**Justice Palace**) **after the Earthquake**
Source: Getty Images

Figure 6.3:   Port-au-Prince Cathedral before the Earthquake
Source: Getty Images

The same is true of the cathedral of Port-au-Prince, a symbol of pride for the Haitians. Figure 6.3 shows the cathedral before the earthquake. The building was severely damaged as the result of the earthquake (see figure 6.4). The cathedral archbishop at the time of the earthquake predicted that it might take more than twenty years before the country could come up with US$30–40 million to rebuild the cathedral and called for parishioners to contribute (Wilentz 2019). Of course, this example has also a lot to do with the complexity of the rebuilding effort and the need for funding. Not all the blame can be laid upon the inefficiency of the national government.

Figure 6.4:   Cathedral of Port-au-Prince Damaged by the Earthquake
Source: Getty Images

New Vulnerabilities

The Haitian population has not yet recovered from the damages and consequences of the earthquake, as evidenced by the household survey conducted for this study. In addition to the survey data, my fieldwork encounters and interviews with Haitian citizens reveal a widespread belief that social and economic conditions have deteriorated since the earthquake. This perception is supported by troubling macroeconomic indicators. According to recent World Bank (2019) data, Haiti has faced a sharp currency depreciation of nearly 30 per cent, inflation rates approaching 20 per cent and a GDP contraction of -0.9 per cent during the 2019 fiscal year.

As a result, Haiti is now even more vulnerable to disasters since no real long-term rehabilitation work was undertaken during the period following the 2010 earthquake, despite foreign interventions and job creation projects. In addressing the question of whether Haiti is now more vulnerable to disasters, Dorvilier, professor of sociology of development at Haiti State University, stressed:

> From an environmental point of view, there are things that have been done, other ways of building, training that have been done. I do not know if we are more vulnerable, but I know that we are still very vulnerable. Vulnerable from the environmental point of view, from floods, erosion, vulnerable to the diseases. We don't have more health centers than before the earthquake, not more sanitation projects in cities where implemented, nor more projects of decongesting urban centers. I think we are as vulnerable, but maybe we made some efforts in terms of awareness of climate hazards, and earthquake hazards.[6]

In other words, even though some things have been done, they have not reduced the vulnerabilities that existed before. This provides the rationale for my thesis: Sustainable development and resilience need to be integrated into rehabilitation and reconstruction efforts. Otherwise, there will be a continuing and perpetual need for disaster relief.

The Project Director at Compassion International argued without equivocation that if another earthquake hits Haiti, there will be considerably more damage. He pointed out that the same building practices are being used as before the earthquake. He attributes this to the Haitian government's failure to enforce building codes. As a result, the pre-existing vulnerabilities remain and even have increased.

As I have argued in chapter 2, even well-intentioned relief efforts may produce new and unforeseen vulnerabilities. This argument has been well-developed by numerous scholars (Delica-Willison and Willison 2008; Hilhorst 2008; Oliver-Smith 2004; Roger 2007). In the case of Haiti, the influx of NGOs in Port-au-Prince became a pull factor for internal migration. In the wake of the earthquake, Port-au-Prince became the centre of aid activities and humanitarian intervention. It was in Port-au-Prince where food distribution activities and the distribution of supplies were centred, where the doctors and nurses who came to provide medical assistance and deliver medications were located and where the NGOs planned the construction of temporary houses for people who had been displaced. People left the rural area and migrated to Port-au-Prince in massive numbers, hoping to benefit from the humanitarian assistance located in the capital city, no matter how inadequate. At the time of the quake, the population of the larger Port-au-Prince area was estimated at 2.1 million inhabitants (ERHW 2020). In 2012, the population increased to 2.4 million (World Population 2020). Today, Port-au-Prince is home to more than 2.7 million Haitians (World Population 2020). With this internal migration, Port-au-Prince – which was already overpopulated – became saturated. Existing slums have grown, and new slums are being built.

New Slums: The Case of Canaan

Problems related to state incapacities have increased vulnerabilities in the post-earthquake period. NGOs may not be able to resolve those problems without collaboration with local governments and organizations. An example that attracted my attention is the creation of Canaan, a new slum near Port-au-Prince. Canaan demonstrates the increased vulnerabilities produced by migration and the failure of NGO intervention in the absence of local government and local organizations.

Canaan was created following the earthquake. In 2016, the population of Canaan was estimated to be two hundred thousand people, and the neighbourhood was rapidly expanding at this time (Meyer-Joassaint 2020). I learned about the community for the first time during an interview with an NGO director. He pointed to the community as an example of new zones of vulnerability created in Port-au-Prince after the earthquake. So I decided to visit Canaan. Immediately upon my arrival, while I was taking pictures, I was advised by a young man to be careful. He pointed to the precarity and uncertainty in the lives of the community's residents and their fears, based on rumours that he repeated, that the state was planning to come in and destroy people's houses. This produced a great degree of hostility directed against the central government. His concern was that people would mistake me for a state official and attack me.

Canaan is a vast community on the northern side of the capital. It is situated on a hill that was almost uninhabited before January 2012. Despite the enormous risks and vulnerabilities, people have chosen to live there because they have no alternatives. The roads are not paved, and there is no running water. Few people have access to electricity, and those who do gain such access do so by illegally running a power line from the closest main street to Canaan.

Canaan differs significantly from Cité Soleil, the largest slum in Port-au-Prince, where people construct makeshift houses. In the latter, the homes are designed to better withstand earthquakes and other catastrophic events due to their makeshift nature. In Canaan, the majority of houses are built with blocks, and a few have concrete roofs, which render them far more vulnerable to destruction and heightens the risk of massive casualties during earthquakes. There is also a considerable risk of potential landslides (see figure 6.5). The community operates outside the jurisdiction of the central government, lacking any municipal authority to address the needs of its residents, enforce codes and regulations or provide services, facilities and infrastructure. It is entirely unregulated.

Figure 6.5:   Photo Exposing the Risk of a Landslide in Canaan[7]
Source: Photo by the Author

NGOs are certainly present in Canaan. They are involved in a project called "Action Plan for Urban Re-structuration". The plan is being funded by Global Communities (an International NGO with its headquarters in Georgia, USA) and the American Red Cross (see figure 6.6). The project was slated to last five months, but was running behind schedule during my visit.. The example of Canaan indicates the failure of the intervention to realize development transformation and how new vulnerabilities can be created despite the presence and involvement of NGOs.

Figure 6.6:   Action Plan for Urban Restructuration of Canaan
Source: Photo by the Author

Ringing the Bell: Public Health and the Next Disaster in Haiti

There are other problems related to the state incapacities that have increased vulnerabilities in the post-earthquake period. A case of concern relates to public health care. There have been significant concerns about public health and sanitation even before the earthquake when more than

80 per cent of health care delivery was provided by NGOs and private individual clinics (Schuller 2012). The earthquake destroyed more of the already limited capacities of the state public health care system, leaving health care delivery almost entirely in the hands of NGOs, whose primary focus is on basic healing, while neglecting prevention, hygiene, personal health practices and other elements that constitute and promote robust public health care delivery. Health delivery worsened after a massive influx of rural migrants, and this caused the population to further depend on medications that were sold on the streets. This was typical even before the earthquake. People who could not afford to see a doctor or go to a pharmacy typically purchased medication based on self-diagnosis, or diagnosis from unlicensed vendors on the streets (see figure 6.7).

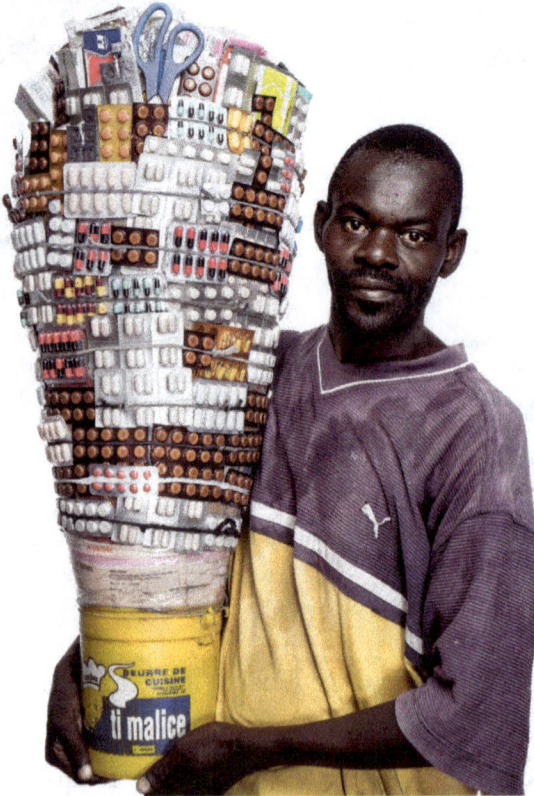

Figure 6.7:   Ady Dumé, 38, Street Medications Vendor
Source: Photo taken by Paolo Woods
The Side Effect/National Geographic

Street medications are less expensive than those sold in pharmacies. Vendors usually get their supplies from black market purchases in the Dominican Republic (Loop 2019). It provides them with a source of income to support their families. With the massive inward migration to Port-au-Prince, the street-medication sales escalated dramatically. These sales exist outside the control of any government authority, are unlicensed and are not reviewed for safety or authenticity.

People also rely on vendors to diagnose their symptoms and prescribe medications. The earthquake contributed significantly to the pre-existing vulnerabilities associated with these practices, which relate to a severe lack of pharmacists in Haiti. According to a 2013 study conducted by the Pharmacist Association of Haiti and the Ministry of Public Health and Population (MSPP), only 676 people worked in the country's pharmaceutical industry. Of these, only 196, representing 29 per cent, had a degree in pharmacy.

This is well below the requirement of twenty-five pharmacists for every ten thousand people that the World Health Organization recommends (Lebrun 2019). Adding to the lack of pharmacists is the lack of state control. Haiti has, in the past, experienced the dire consequence of a lack of control when it comes to medications. In 1996, contaminated medications[8] caused acute kidney failure among children. About two hundred children lost their lives, and more than twenty became physically and mentally disabled (Fils-Aimé 2018). The combination of a lack of pharmacists and the absence of state control of the practice facilitated the illicit sale of medications by street vendors.

Vulnerabilities related to public health are also exacerbated by the deplorable sanitary conditions in the country that worsened as a result of the earthquake. Mountains of trash are everywhere. In the public market, street vendors sell their groceries and cooked food near piles of garbage. During a focus group with *Sove Fanm* (Save the Women), a women's organization, the severity of the problem was raised as a central concern, particularly as it pertained to young, poor women in the country. These included problems related to basic hygiene, such as washing hands after using the bathroom, a practice that is not always followed in poor communities because of the absence of the facilities to do so. The inability to adhere to such practices was one of the reasons that explained the post-earthquake cholera outbreak, which caused more than eight thousand seven hundred deaths (Passport Health 2015).

Also, Haiti has the second-highest rate of HIV prevalence in the world for any country outside of Africa (Hintzen 2019; PANCAP 2017; UNAIDS Secretariat; The World Bank 2005). This is explained by the combined effects of extreme poverty, poor access to health care and structural vulnerabilities stemming from an ineffective government that make Haiti's population extremely vulnerable to epidemics.

These vulnerabilities related to inadequacies of the health care system that were exacerbated by the earthquake provide examples of the problem of state incapacity and reliance on NGOs. NGOs cater primarily to basic healing and ignore the fundamental conditions to ensure resilience, prevention and robust recovery through a vibrant public health system. The lack of capacity, the state's incapability and its absence at the local level have contributed to practices that heighten risk, vulnerability and precarity. NGOs, while active, are often unable to address these issues in ways that yield sustainable outcomes – nor is this typically within their mandate. As such, the solution lies in fostering a dynamic and effective collaboration between NGOs and local governments or community-based organizations. The example of Canaan demonstrates the increased vulnerabilities produced by migration and the failure of NGO intervention in the absence of local government and local organizations.

Summary

In this chapter, I argued that the goals established and the commitments made at the International Donors' Conference have not been realized ten years after the earthquake. One of the examples of the unrealized goals and promises that I mentioned relates to the major government buildings that have yet to be repaired or rebuilt. As a result of the intervention's failure to achieve its development goals, new vulnerabilities have emerged while existing ones have been further exacerbated. The sale of medications on the streets of Port-au-Prince and the construction of Canaan are examples of such failure. The state's incapacities can explain this failure, but it is largely due to the ineffectiveness of the disaster intervention. The solution is NGO collaboration with local governments and organizations as an alternative. Particularly, the example of Canaan demonstrates the increased vulnerabilities produced by migration and the failure of NGO intervention in the absence of local government and local organizations.

SEVEN

Unending Relief and Increased Vulnerabilities

In the end, we will conserve only what we love; we will love only what we understand, and we will understand only what we are taught.

Baba Dioum, Senegalese forestry engineer

Nations can overcome the forms of disjuncture that foster precarity and vulnerability by investing in human development. The central argument of this book, therefore, is that for disaster aid to effectively reduce vulnerability and build resilience, it must be aligned with broader development goals. Generally, disaster intervention focuses its efforts on three types of activities: relief, rehabilitation and reconstruction (Christoplos 2006; Dube 2020; Mosel and Levine 2014; Ramet 2012). The first type, relief efforts (also called "emergency aid") aims to save lives, prevent a worsening of the impact of the disaster and bring aid to victims (Riddell 2008). The second type, rehabilitation, focuses on helping people and restoring conditions of habitability and is often seen as a bridge between relief and development (Buchanan-Smith and Maxwell 1994; Dube 2020; Ramet 2012). It allows people to regain their functionality and rebuild their lives. As such, it aims to reorganize administrative, sanitary and governmental structures (Mosel and Levine 2014). And the third type engages the reconstruction process. The goal of reconstruction is to rebuild the physical infrastructure. This phase can open up opportunities for corrective measures by building more resilient and sustainable infrastructures (Dube 2020).

Haiti's post-disaster response prioritized relief and paid less attention to rehabilitation and reconstruction. Things have still not returned to normal, as I have demonstrated in chapter 5. The intervention has, therefore, failed. There are three reasons for this failure: 1) inadequate efforts to increase the capacities of people and reduce their vulnerability, 2) lack of collaboration between the NGOs and local governments and 3) state inefficiency.

Inadequate Efforts to Increase Capacities and Reduce Vulnerabilities

Based on the institutional ethnography of three NGOs and the in-depth, semi-structured interviews that I conducted, it becomes evident that the explanation for the failure of recovery efforts is that Haiti's disaster response efforts were not designed to undertake sustainable interventions that could have long-term outcomes. This particularly relates to the way funding was allocated for the intervention. Much of the funding was allocated for relief activities. In chapter 2, I raised the possibility of linking relief to development. Such possibilities were not thoroughly considered by NGOs because they think that long-term outcomes are outside their mandate.

I conducted institutional ethnographies of three NGOs (see table 7.1) that are engaged in relief work in Haiti to assess the reasons why recovery efforts failed and to examine practices that offer possibilities for sustainable interventions.

Mr Laurent, a former UN consultant in Haiti with experience in relief interventions across several African countries, and serving as an NGO consultant in Haiti during my fieldwork, explained in an interview the inherent challenges of integrating sustainability efforts into relief operations:

> If I am the director of an emergency aid non-governmental organization, my mandate is to respond to an emergency. An emergency, what is it for an emergency organization? It's that you have a baseline. Take, for example, Cite Soleil! We have a baseline made up of social, health, economic and security data, etc. And we know about the normal situation based on statistical data. Me as an emergency NGO, I will not intervene

Table 7.1: List of NGOs, Field of Intervention and Philosophy

NGO	Type	Field of Intervention	Location	Mission/ Philosophy
Cooperazione Internationale (COOPI)	Non-Religious	Infrastructure, Disaster Prevention and Preparedness	Tabarre, Cité Soleil, Port-au-Prince	Supporting communities for recovery and long-lasting development
Compassion International	Religious	Education, Micro-finance,	Carrefour/ Delmas, Port-au-Prince, Cite Soleil	Release children from poverty
GOAL Global	Non-Religious	Development, Environment, Infrastructure	Port-au-Prince	To create safe and resilient communities. Bringing lasting change to improve the lives of Haitians

on a problem that is a global issue, political economy, social, that is from the realm of substantive sustainable intervention ... On the other hand, if there is an earthquake, all the data are collapsed; here I am going to intervene. I will intervene because it is my mandate. I am responding to an emergency because this baseline has been broken. There is a break, and this rupture puts people's lives in danger. And here I intervene. I intervene so that there are fewer possible deaths, fewer possible injuries and to try to place back the line that was fractured. At the level of a long-term intervention, it is not my level as an emergency organization that this baseline that we are trying to upgrade, it's not good as an emergency NGO to do it. I do not have the capacity. I do not have the resources, I cannot afford it and it's not my mandate.[1]

Mr Laurent is referring to a reality of relief organizations and relief efforts, the fact that sustainable interventions are not built into their mandate. As emergency relief NGOs, their mandates are to save lives, feed the hungry, provide temporary shelters and the like. Mr Laurent compared the situation of Haiti in the aftermath of the earthquake to an individual who had a heart attack. Emergency assistance was called. The goal of the emergency team is, at this point, only to save the life of the patient. If the team arrives and does just that, their mission is over. Mr Laurent says:

> In case of a catastrophe, the impact of the response is immediate. I take the example of a medical NGO; you have a patient who is walking from home to go to work. And suddenly she/he has a cardiovascular attack. The emergency response is that you have a team that comes in, takes the issue in charge, revives the patient, stabilizes him or her and takes the patient to the hospital. Once the patient is revived, the emergency work is over, and you have saved that life. But then there is much work to do. What are the causes of this cardiac arrest? And it is not the emergency team that will work on it. They do not have the capacity, the memory or the knowledge to investigate the cause of this cardiovascular event. You will have in front of you a professional in cardiology who will have to do analysis, who will treat the problem and increase the resilience of his patient, to ask him to follow a treatment that will be identifiable, by analysing what the person has suffered in his heart, if it is necessary to schedule an operation in a year or two, etc. And one is in the increase in the resilience of the patient. And this is done over a year or two years. While the emergency response is done in an hour or two.

The point Mr Laurent is making here is that emergency medical response personnel do not have the capabilities and capacities needed for rehabilitation. It is the work of another team of specialists who engage in rehabilitation and long-term outcomes.

The reality is that many relief organizations continued to work in Haiti, years after the earthquake. Some of them were still there ten years after the earthquake. This explains, partly, Haiti's failure to recover, given the almost exclusive focus on relief. This exclusive focus on relief was exemplified in the long-term practices of GOAL Global,[2] an international humanitarian NGO founded in Ireland over forty years ago. GOAL launched an emergency intervention in Haiti immediately following the earthquake that was still ongoing at the time that I conducted my study, ten years later. One of GOAL's high-ranking officers explained the situation in this way:

> Moreover, there was the whole issue of emergency projects that were not intended to bring lasting results but, first of all, to immediately bring help. Mainly, I think all the emergency interventions that we still see five

years after, you should know that these programmes were not planned to last five years, but because of the stagnation of the situation, those things remain.[3]

The need for disaster relief will continue to persist because people's lives and well-being continue to be at risk. In addition, the recurrence of disasters is so pervasive that it has become the standardized practice for NGOs to be perpetually moving from one location to another in order to replicate their efforts of disaster relief. For example, during my fieldwork in Haiti, GOAL was about to move to Jérémie, the southwest side of the country, to implement the same project that they had implemented in Port-au-Prince. Jérémie was severely hit by hurricane Matthew (World Bank Group 2017). This hurricane struck the south and southwest side of the country in the Fall of 2016, leaving more than 1.4 million people in need of humanitarian assistance and around two hundred thousand homes damaged (World Bank Group 2017).

Some emergency agencies that were in Haiti as a result of the earthquake left because they did not see their mission in terms of the long-haul or building resilience. What is indicated here is a clear need for NGOs and other types of interventions to support programmes and projects for substantive sustainable development. Without these efforts, there would be a perpetual need for disaster relief in the face of the common recurrence of catastrophic events in Haiti. I am arguing here for development – for a better approach to build efforts to reduce vulnerability and increase resilience. This approach requires two things: 1) for the increase of funding for development agencies and 2) for resilience to be integrated into programmes and projects related to disaster intervention.

Increase Funding for Development Agencies

The question of funding remained a recurrent theme in the interviews and focus groups that I conducted. Even though there was a significant influx of emergency NGOs in the wake of the earthquake, there was little money allocated to efforts aimed at sustainable intervention. The CLIO's resilience committee chair put it in this way:

> Many NGOs are in the humanitarian response. Because for a country like Haiti, it is difficult to have an emergency and then not to come. This will discredit you as an organization in front of the population, because you are supposed to help. So, as you come in for the response, you therefore automatically enter the humanitarian response.[4]

Notwithstanding the fact of intervention, it is the structure of the response that contributes to the persistence of the crisis leading to the need for additional relief efforts. The main explanation for the way in which the response is organized is that donors fund short-term projects, which makes it difficult for agencies to implement projects with possible long-term outcomes. Mr Laurent explains it:

> Concerning the fund that is allocated to emergency organizations, the major emergency donors, from my point of view, require a few things impossible to achieve. If you take the main emergency donors like ECHO from the European Union, you notice that their funding for the emergency response is in very short cycles. In general, most contracts that are signed between these emergency donors and emergency NGOs are contracts of twelve months to eighteen months.[5] Even for development NGOs who receive funding for more sustainable projects, a cycle of twelve to eighteen months comes with significant problems.

Mr Laurent continues:

> It is extremely difficult, if not impossible, to develop global resilience capacities after the earthquake in a capital like Port-au-Prince in eighteen months. It is an impossible mission. I could give you two or three examples of European NGOs that have benefited from the funds to rebuild, improve homes, so they resist cyclones, that was in the *Nippes*. And at the end of the twelve-month project, the organization was unable to build the five hundred houses for which it received funding. Why? Because it's impossible to do that in twelve months and even in eighteen.

> … So, there is also this contradiction, there is a strong demand from all the donors of the global system on the emergency NGOs by telling them you must identify this response that allows you to develop these resilience capacities. Even if the financial resources are there, the mechanisms of these contracts and the donors very often do not give these organizations the time necessary to develop these strategies.[6]

NGOs were forced to focus on humanitarian projects because that is where the money was. Even NGOs that work in the area of development were forced to focus particularly on humanitarian projects for which funding was easier to receive. This was the case for the *Cooperazione Internazionale* (COOPI), an Italian NGO that works both in emergencies and development. According to its website, "COOPI operates in contexts of extreme poverty and socio-political or environmental vulnerability implementing the Linking Relief, Rehabilitation and Development (LRRD) approach. This gives COOPI the chance to provide sustainable and long-term responses, ensuring continuity between security, humanitarian aid and development" (COOPI Website).

One of the high-ranking officials of COOPI in Haiti at the time of my fieldwork described a project that her organization was working on:

> We also work at cite Soleil. Cite Soleil is an extremely vulnerable area (see figure 7.1). And here, for example, we intervene with cash for work. Cash for work, and the works we were targeting were cleaning the canals. This cleaning of the canals was done with the Municipality. We sat down with the mayors and asked what areas are you targeting that need more cleaning. The mayors and with some other leaders decided[7] that it was Drouillard. The Drouillard project, we started working in the area, we did cash for work, 120 people for fifteen days to clean the area. This is really an emergency, an emergency intervention. What happens in these areas is that almost every time there is an hour of rain, even if it is not too heavy, the days after there is a flood in these areas.[8]

The COOPI's official also added:

> Significant intervention is required. We did a cash for work; it was a punctual action to help out the situation a bit, but I assure you that a week after or a few days after the area will be as it was.[9]

The point of this is that, even for an NGO whose focus is on sustainability, resources prevent long-term responses, leading to a concentration on stopgap short-term measures.

When I asked the COOPI's official why she is not looking to get funding for a more sustainable project, she replied that it was not easy because the United Nations aid-funding programme often decides their priorities, which may not be for something sustainable. Therefore, there is a need to extend the timeframe for the projects because the need continues beyond the normal funding cycle. Mostly there is a need to divert money towards more sustainable projects and to development agencies capable of building resilience.

Figure 7.1:   Drainage Filled with Debris and Trash Near Cité Soleil[10]
Source: Photo by the Author

Building Resilience into Projects

In chapter 2, I have argued that resilience allows communities to recover in the wake of a disaster quickly. Resilience can be built when a system can withstand a disaster or is able to recover rapidly after a disaster has occurred. For example, building a bridge to repair a road allows the road to return to use immediately after a disaster has occurred.

It is clear that resilience was not built into the post-disaster response efforts in Haiti. There was unanimous agreement among the NGO officials interviewed that disaster intervention did not increase resilience to disasters in Haiti. There are at least two reasons that explain this failure: 1) a lack of collaboration between NGOs and the local governments and 2) a disjuncture between humanitarian efforts, rehabilitation and the construction phase.

Lack of Collaboration between Aid Agencies/NGOs and Local Governments

International funding agencies have been reluctant to involve local governments and have not supported their efforts to be involved in post-disaster relief. This has been the case even when local officials were approached. This can be explained partly by decisions by funders to bypass national and local authorities because of corruption, inefficiency and inefficacy, as previously discussed. When they do this, funds are usually allocated to the central government and expended in ways that deny local authorities the capacity to implement sustainable programmes and projects.

The municipality of Delmas is the richest municipality in Port-au-Prince, but not the municipality where the wealthiest Haitians live. Their riches are due to a history of strong and dynamic local government that has the capacity to collect taxes and invest in municipal infrastructure. In my interview with two officials from the municipality of Delmas, they stated that Delmas is better prepared than any other city in the country to respond to and mitigate the impact of the next future disaster. The municipality has better hospitals, more equipment and an administration that functions better than other municipalities in Port-au-Prince. The two officials explained that in cases of emergencies in neighboring municipalities, such as fires, they often rely on the municipality of Delmas for assistance. However, Delmas's resources are limited, and municipalities frequently find themselves appealing to NGOs for support.

There are hurdles, however, that often obstruct the local governments in the country from getting this kind of assistance.[11] A mayor that I interviewed during my fieldwork explained some frustration at this level. The mayor explained to me that the European Union (EU) has begun a process to fund development projects by channelling funds to some municipalities of Port-au-Prince. The EU conducted many workshops with the mayors regarding the funding process. The mayors were asked to bring their projects to be evaluated. However, the EU abruptly halted the process, evoking the legal difficulty that they may face if circumventing the central government and working directly with the local government.

There is a need for new policies that could allow multilateral and international agencies, particularly NGOs, to work directly with local governments. In this perspective, this book is advocating for devolution, the process through which the central government transfers more responsibilities to local governments for the control, development and support of public policy (Crowe et al. 2015; Willett 2016). Devolution can allow local governments to negotiate with international partners and make development decisions according to the need of their communities and the availability of resources.

It has been demonstrated that in developed countries, devolution has led to a more sustainable system of governance (Willett 2016). Parallelly, highly centralized governments in Third World countries have often led to weak, inefficient and unequitable distribution of resources (Bossert 1998; Barker et al. 2014). In the case of Haiti, where the central government is weak and inefficient, devolution could be a path for dynamic local governments to create possibilities for genuine development while receiving NGO assistance and funding.

In addition to local government, there are also national and local organizations that INGOs could partner with in order to implement projects capable of producing long-term development transformation. Those national and local organizations have been largely excluded in post disaster response in Haiti. In the case of Haiti, there are credible organizations that are working in the communities. They develop social programmes that can reduce poverty, they engage in microfinance, education, health care delivery and the like. If INGOs work closely with those local organizations, provide funding and increase their capacities, the outcomes will be tremendously positive. Many social and economic projects in Haiti are implemented by and through local churches. NGOs could be partnered with those local churches that have a proven record in the communities to build long-term sustainable projects. When those projects are implemented by the local organizations, by the people and with the people, using local resources, and when the ownership is created, built and solidified, the projects will go beyond the presence of the NGOs. When the NGOs leave, the projects will survive. That is how sustainable development is built.

The practice by official funding agencies of excluding the participation of national and local organizations in the post-disaster response goes a long way in explaining the 2010 post-disaster intervention in Haiti. This was pointed out by Mr Laurent in our interview:

> At the national level, you have capacities within the civil society, local organizations which could very well acquire these capacities for emergency response, but they are not. Then, you have to pose the problem of access to funding that allows the local organizations to develop these capacities. National organizations often have a great deal of difficulty to have access to these funds which can allow them, on the one hand, to prepare and, on the other hand, to respond. They are not very often eligible for funding from emergency donors.[12]

As argued in chapter 4, national and local agencies are often more effective than international ones. They possess a deeper understanding of local realities and are generally more cost-effective in their management and operations. There are problems related to the high costs associated with the payment of international consultants and expatriates to implement a project that can be reduced significantly by the employment of nationals. There are also problems related to unfamiliarity with local policies and official and unofficial practices and arrangements. During the institutional ethnography of GOAL, I observed the implementation of a rebuilding project in *Turgeau* in a neighbourhood in the commune of Port-au-Prince (see figure 7.2). About US$2.5 million was spent on the project, but not many houses were repaired or rebuilt. A director of GOAL implicitly expressed his uneasiness with the failure of the project to fully and efficiently realize its stated goals:

> We were able to work on eighty houses. It is not much in an area that may have two thousand five hundred houses. We were stuck on the issue of land rights. Perhaps 70 per cent of the area has been declared out of bounds due to land issues. It was difficult. This has limited our interventions from small pockets at the accommodation level. And we made eighty houses which are validated by the engineers, good structure etc.... For these eighty houses it works, on the other hand it costs us a lot of money for eighty houses. I don't know if this is the solution for all our problems.[13]

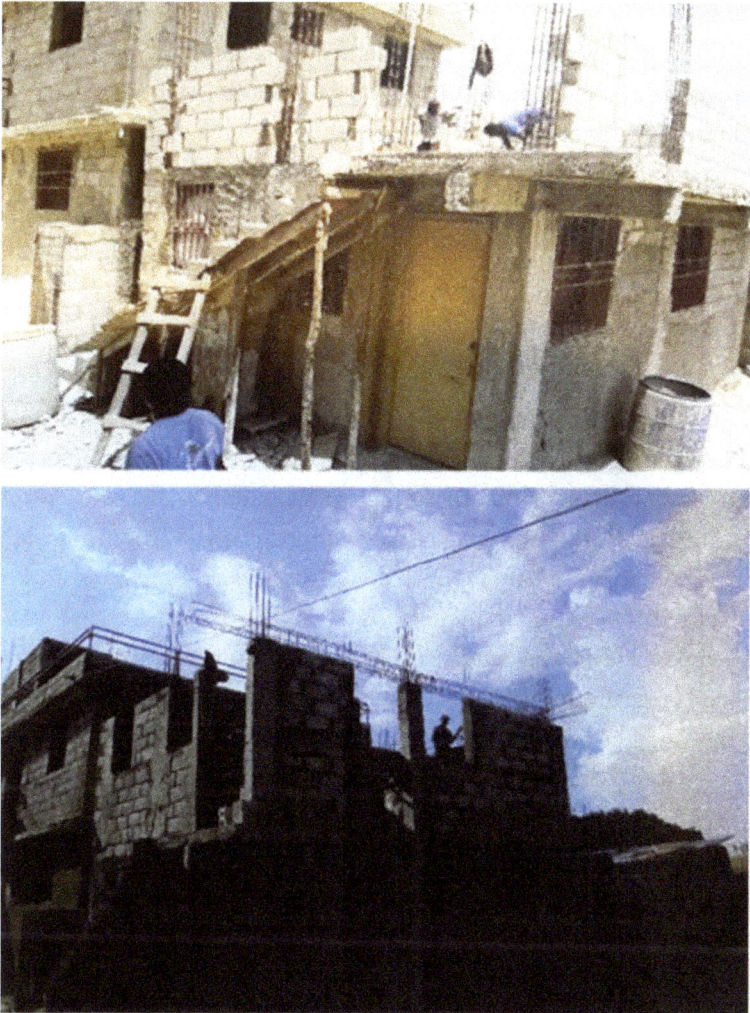

Figure 7.2:   Homes Built by GOAL Global in Turgeau, Port-au-Prince
Source: Photos by the Author

The issue of the land rights that he mentions is a very complicated one in Haiti. Many homeowners have no land title. While some people build on family land (without any land title), many often build on a piece of land that they rent from a landowner with the possibility for the homeowner to buy in the future if the landowner decides to sell. The law does not fully protect the homeowner against the landowner in case the homeowner is not able to purchase when the landowner decides to sell.

It becomes clear that the poor performance in efforts to implement the project and in the realization of its deliverables is a result of the lack of knowledge of the structural problems as they relate to land issues in *Turgeau* and the transactional cost of the project. Much of these could have been resolved by the participation of a local NGO familiar with land issues and where costs could have been significantly reduced. More houses would have been repaired or rebuilt.

Relief and Sustainable Development

Sustainable development needs to be incorporated into emergency relief planning. There is a need to implement in disaster relief effort the coordinated sequential incorporation of rehabilitation and reconstruction in order to ensure sustainable recovery and resilience. This can be done through effective collaboration between donors and local institutions but also between international NGOs and local institutions, which encompass local governments, NGOs and other local stakeholders and agencies. Ideally, local institutions are more informed of the reality on the ground, the eventual challenges that the response may face, and how to solve those challenges. It also requires aid agencies and international NGOs to build local capacities and strengthen relationships with local institutions and organizations by showing a greater capacity to manage. Capacity building can be formed when aid agencies channel money through those organizations and when NGOs work jointly with them. The benefit of such an approach is that real issues will be tackled with fewer external resources, which will result in greater outcomes.

Also significant for rehabilitation and the reconstruction process is to attack the structural conditions that make people vulnerable in the first place. For example, it requires new housing models and styles that can resist an earthquake in the case of Haiti, a proper drainage system capable of mitigating the consequence of a flood, bridges and roads that are easy to make and to rebuild in the advent of a disaster, resilient healthcare based on prevention and cost-effective care, and the development of an efficient social management system through a dynamic collaboration between NGOs and local government. Such social management requires agencies to work toward mitigating risks and preventing the next disaster.

I discussed the idea of linking relief with development in chapter 2. As difficult as such a linking may be to put into practice, there is considerable evidence of its feasibility. Fritz Dorvilier, sociologist and professor at Haiti State University, thinks that the two are complementary. He said:

> We must reconcile the two. Education is a development factor. If we send a child to school, the child cannot learn if he is hungry, we cannot make this child a development actor tomorrow. He will not be able to graduate. He will drop out of school, or he will learn poorly, he will not be able to participate in development. But if there is occasional help which provides a school canteen, then the child will be able to learn better in school. At that point we can reconcile humanitarian aid and development, we can reconcile the school canteen, the uniform, the shoes, and building a new school for children. So the schools that were degraded, destroyed by the earthquake, if we had humanitarian aid that builds those schools, even if it is occasional aid, it is humanitarian aid, of short duration, but the school, infrastructure will last, education will last for generations, etc. When there is a famine somewhere in the rural area and help is provided, instead of the population of this area migrating to Port-au-Prince they stay since aid is provided to them. If the population migrates to Port-au-Prince, they will swell the slums, their vulnerability will increase, there will be violence, banditry, and insecurity. But if we provide some help to these people there, they will be able to cross the impasse, the impasse of famine. At that time, we will give them food, seeds, and tools. It is humanitarian aid but at the same time, the children are trained, schools are built at the same time, we give them occasional help, but at the same time we help to plant, we help them to develop small businesses, to develop skills in different areas. At that time, we reconcile humanitarian aid to development.[14]

The political economist, Abnel Désamours, attempted to solve the issue differently. He considered not whether emergency relief and development can be linked, but rather how emergency relief can be provided in other ways to contribute to development:

> I believe that the activities listed in the case of emergency interventions, these activities ... we can do humanitarian work at the same time as we do the structural. For example, when using cash for work for sanitation activities, I think that when spending huge funds on sanitation, I am not saying that sanitation activities are not important, but if with this money we use it either to facilitate the construction of these irrigation canals, or for the rehabilitation of watersheds to reduce our economic

vulnerability if this money is used for this purpose we can reconcile emergency assistance and the long-term. What is the objective? It is to allow individuals to recover their livelihood following a disaster. When they are employed in such activities, they earn a little income, now the whole question is, what are we going to employ them for? Are we going to use them to solve problems that are likely to strengthen the economy, and which are likely to strengthen the productive apparatus or reduce environmental vulnerability?[15]

State Inefficiency and Lack of Coordination

In chapter 5, I argued that for disaster aid to be effective, in the absence of an effective and efficient state, aid needs to be channeled through local government and organizations. There are strategies that can be pursued at the local level to ensure resilience, such as for NGOs and funders to work with local organizations and local authorities. Regardless of whether development NGOs are in charge of the intervention, it would be difficult for such intervention to be successful without the critical involvement and guidance of the state or the local government and authorities. Mr Laurent put it this way:

> Other donors who are development donors like the European Commission, USAID, these donors have the contractual possibilities much more important in terms of amount and much more important in terms of duration, which can go up to four years, up to five years. And there you can effectively develop strategies that will allow an urban city like Port-au-Prince to develop something with the populations but also with the authorities, with the state. Because we cannot develop systems in an urban area like Port-au-Prince that can improve the resilience of urban populations without the necessary implications of the administrative authorities that manage things.[16]

Mr Laurent's argument implies that sustainable intervention can be done through effective local administrations. The essential role of the state is to make such cooperation possible. The local administration needs to create the necessary infrastructure and make policies that facilitate the cooperation between local organizations/governments and NGOs.[17]

With effective cooperation between the local authorities and NGOs, both rehabilitation and reconstruction can occur simultaneously. There are multiple examples of successes resulting from such cooperation. A meaningful example of the successes following a disaster occurred when Typhoon Morakot hit Taiwan in August 2009, causing major damage, including a serious landslide. As a result of a dynamic collaboration between NGOs and a capable state, an efficient post-disaster response was implemented. The collaboration allowed the successful task of reconstruction to begin two weeks after the disaster (Chern and Liu 2014). Although in the case of Typhoon Morakot's post-disaster intervention, the response was done under the guidance of an effective state, there was a strong presence of the local governments in the management and implementation of the response.

Jeen-Chuan Chern and Ching-Tsung Liu (2014) report that during the phase of reconstruction, the central government made the policy directives, prepared the budget, provided the land for the reconstruction, and undertook the reconstruction of public places, while the responsibility of the management of the reconstruction and decision on the policies for future maintenance and management was undertaken by the local governments. The NGOs were instructed to build private permanent housing. Under the coordination of the government, they built permanent houses by districts. The government decided on the timeline and the style for the housing reconstruction, and the organization was entrusted with implementing the work by districts.

All the issues regarding rezoning, land acquisition and compensation, and negotiation with landowners were cleared with the government to facilitate the building agencies' work. With such coordination, the rehabilitation and the reconstruction occurred rapidly. In the Tzu Chi Da-ai community, for example, with the coordination of the local government, an agency completed the first phase of a project by building more than six hundred houses within six months following the typhoon.

Chern and Liu (2014) point out that two years after the catastrophic event, about 90 per cent of the total required houses were already completed. All the other work of rehabilitation, such as road paving, fixing streetlights and installing running water, were implemented mainly by the government immediately after the construction was over. In addition to the government intervention, NGOs assisted in building disaster-resilient bridges, managing rivers and implementing industrial activities that created long-term employment opportunities for the residents.

Such collaboration was lacking in the post-disaster intervention in Haiti. The incapacities and ineffectual nature of the state prevented any chance at collaboration with NGOs, which is a necessary condition for success. Indeed, since the earthquake, the state has become even more ineffectual and less reliable as a partner. NGOs have resorted to replicating their efforts in response to new disasters. This acts to the detriment of recovery efforts, preventing and forestalling successful rehabilitation.

Another example of how state inefficiency and incapacity reduce NGOs' chances for success relates to the fact that state presence is almost nonexistent in many local communities, even when for the purpose of law enforcement. This has significant negative effects on the ability of NGOs to function. A high-ranking staff member at Compassion International emphasized this point by pointing out the organization's inability to build safer houses. This is because, in the face of the absence of the state, unregulated squatting and building is rampant, creating serious exposure to risk and safety concerns. These could be resolved at the local level. He expressed his frustration in this term:

> The state is not a state that takes responsibility for enforcing construction norms and standards; there is not a construction plan. If there is something on paper, they do not apply it. Because of that, people build anywhere and anyhow. There is no inspection before once starts building, no local authority to tell you if you can build or not. People have built near the ravine, with no water, no road, no norms to follow, which places the country in a situation of chaos. No matter what state, how it is built, or where it is built, the state does not have such control capacity. Everyone lives and expects anything, anytime, may happen.[18]

The solution here is to provide the capabilities at the local level to local authorities. NGOs are not opposed to a form of oversight. Instead, they share the idea that in order to function effectively, they must collaborate with and be guided by state policy and practice. In an ideal situation, this would be their preference. They are pointing out the problems posed by an ineffectual and inefficient state that is not present. Joseph (Interview

2018), the president of a US-based charity that funds college education in Haiti, expressed his frustration by complaining about the lack of state guidance to direct the charity's interventions. There were no officials available to point them to where the needs were. He complained that as a result, "people come out and do it on their own, and they come down saying we will help do this for you, and the Haitians said go ahead, do it". The point is that, in the absence of a compelling state presence, NGOs must depend on local participation.

He also expressed his deep frustration with corruption. Small charities (like Joseph's Friend of Haiti), which do not have the same name, protection, or notoriety as the "big NGOs", find themselves without protection from the pervasive demands for bribery or corrupt demands from officials. As an example, they are often forced to pay money under the table at customs to get their belongings, supplies and aid packages that they bring for the country. This is another impediment.

The issues of incapacity, inefficiency and corruption at all levels of government come with severe consequences relating to decisions for NGOs to operate in the country. In the absence of an effective and efficient state presence, some NGOs are finding ways to engage in good practices and projects effectively and efficiently with long-term positive outcomes. It is essential to share a few examples of these as well.

Between Frustration and Hope

Despite their frustrations, NGOs are providing effective services in many areas, which gives hope for the future. Many are successfully implementing and running projects that can produce long-term positive outcomes and increase people's capabilities and resilience. One example is a school rebuilding project funded by the Compassion International NGO for at least thirty schools damaged by the earthquake.

The decision was made from the start to build school structures in ways that satisfy seismic standards and are hurricane and cyclone-resistant (See figure 7.3). The structures can also be used as shelters in case of a potentially disastrous natural event. While not many schools have been rebuilt, this project is an example of good practices that can be replicated elsewhere. Two other projects that I researched during my fieldwork provide similar examples of success and good practices that are sustainable by building the capacities of the community stakeholders. One that was previously mentioned was designed by Compassion International as an income-generating strategy, and the other as an emergency and disaster preparedness project implemented by the COOPI. These two case studies are presented below.

Figure 7.3:   School of Eglise Baptiste de Salem[19]
Source: Photo by the Author

Case Study One: Building Economic Capacities

Project: Income Generation Activities (IGA).

This programme was designed to help beneficiaries open small businesses or expand a previous business by providing low-interest loans at 12 per cent annual interest rates, "which was far better than the other IGA organizations where loan interest rates can reach as high as 40 per cent" (Interview with project manager, Compassion International 2018). The programme started in 2010 and ended in 2014. Initially, the programme intended to provide over US$1 million in loans to a total of one thousand individuals. As requirements to apply for the programme, applicants need to take basic business planning training offered by Compassion International and submit a business plan with the loan application. Approved applicants received the loan. The programme trained approximately 1,250 individuals, provided more than US$1.2 million, facilitated the creation of 453 businesses and created possibly thousands of new jobs. The programme stopped providing new loans in early 2014.

Discussion

The Compassion International Income Generating Activities programme directly attacks the root causes of people's material and financial vulnerabilities, which include income depletion, unemployment and lack of access to financial services. It resolves these problems by increasing its recipients' capacities, providing financial training, ensuring relatively long-term financial stability for recipients and their households and creating jobs. Five years after the programme ended, many of those small businesses still existed.

I interviewed the project manager. He praised the programme's success and emphasized its practice of working with the recipients, giving them advice on how to grow their businesses, and empowering women and young people. Many of the beneficiaries were young individuals (Interview with project manager, Compassion International 2018).

So it was important for me to meet with some beneficiaries of the programme and visit them in my efforts to evaluate the success of the programme. I met with five beneficiaries who shared their assessment with me. In figure 7.4, I present a shoe store that I visited. This business was created through a grant from the programme. One loan recipient, for example, was able to use the earnings from his resuscitated business to rebuild his house, which had been damaged in the earthquake, through the programme. After the earthquake, he lost his business, a tailor shop. With the loan from Compassion International, he was able to reopen his shop and rebuild his house later on. I visited the shop. During our conversation, he shared with me that without this money, he would not have been able to get back on his feet. He wished that a programme like this would continue so more people could benefit from it.

The programme was relatively successful despite facing many fundamental problems, particularly the management of the portfolio and accounting systems. The problems are largely because the organization had no history and background in this type of activity or microfinance and did not have an existing organizational infrastructure to deliver these services. These problems were particularly evident when the programme was first implemented.

In 2016, after Hurricane Matthew devastated the southern part of the country, the programme was reproduced in Les Cayes. By the time the project was successfully reproduced in Les Cayes, these problems had been largely overcome.

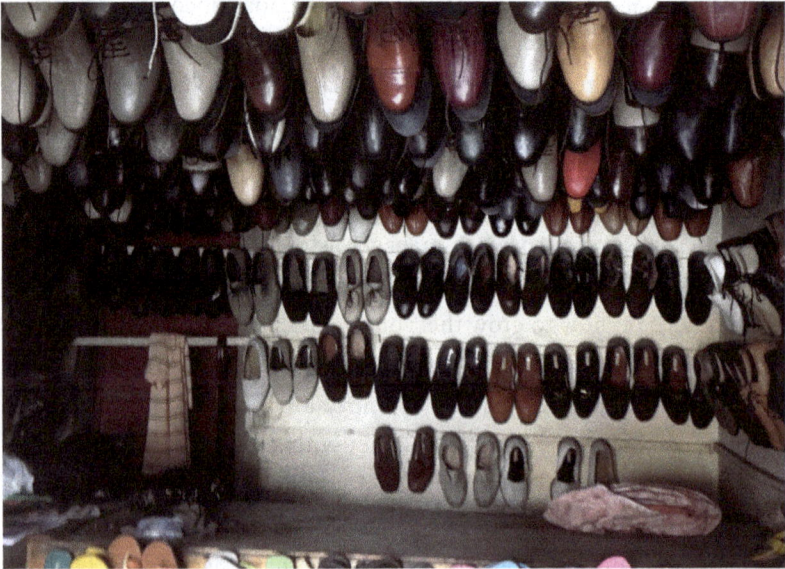

Figure 7.4: Shoe Shop of a Compassion International IGA Programme Beneficiary
Source: *Photo by the Author*

Case Study Two: Disaster Prevention and Preparedness

Project: Enhancing physical and social capital at the neighbourhood level for disaster preparedness, emergency reaction capacities and preventive territorial management.

The objective of this project was to reduce the impact of disasters by improving collective infrastructures through small-scale mitigation works for Disaster Risk Reduction (DRR). The project was implemented in 2018 in Tabarre and Cité Soleil, neighbourhoods of the greater Port-au-Prince that used to be part of the municipality of Delmas. In Cité Soleil, the project consisted of cleaning the drainage canals. In Tabarre, the project involved constructing walking bridges that linked neighbourhoods that were inaccessible when it rains, "improving disaster preparedness response among the most vulnerable through disaster drills" (COOPI Project Report) and strengthening local government DRR capacity. The projects built more than twelve walking bridges and distributed emergency kits to many families. With the collaboration of the mayors and the municipality leaders, they established a disaster department in the municipality of Tabarre.

Discussion

As I have indicated in an earlier reference to this project, the lack of funding severely affected the successful implementation of one aspect of the project, forcing the substitution of the cleaning of the drainage canal system in Cité Soleil for the building of a new one. Where the project succeeded was in the construction of bridges, which aimed "at mitigating the population exposure to risks by addressing difficulties in mobility, lack of knowledge and capacities of communities, public and private local actors on how to mitigate and respond to natural disasters and poor waste management" (COOPI Website). In particular, the bridges were built to facilitate the neighbouring population's crossing from one community to the next, which was difficult when it was raining and caused serious risk exposures.

More significant, however, was the organizational structure of the project rather than its content. First, the project involved the community in every aspect of its implementation. It utilized a grassroots strategy by working within the community, helping stakeholders to organize themselves and creating a structure that had the potential to mitigate damage in case of an unfortunate event. Secondly, the project developed a dynamic collaboration with the local government. The administrative structure for disaster prevention and mitigation is poorly organized in Haiti, especially at the municipality level. The chief administrator, who is responsible for civil protection in the municipality, is the mayor. COOPI, through this project, created a dynamic relationship with the commune's administrative leadership by providing them with the tools and resources to create a disaster department in the city and by helping them create a budget. The department undertook the task of working with the NGO to mitigate risks and intervene in the case of a catastrophic event. In my interview with Sofia (personal communication 2018), a high-ranking foreign official of COOPI at the time of my fieldwork, she stressed this point:

> I say that mayors need to get involved in the process. The more the mayors get involved, the more positive the response, the stronger the civil perception, the structure, and so on. The less the mayors get involved, the less it is structured.[20]

Thirdly, the project mobilized and empowered women in the community. These women formed an organization called the *Regroupment des Femmes Professionelles en Construction* (RFPCH) (Group of Professional Women in Construction). They were mobilized to participate in the construction of the bridges in Tabarre. After constructing the bridges, a committee was formed to ensure bridge maintenance. The committee integrated both men and women. Finally, the bridges were easy to repair and replace. In case of a potential disaster, the community has the training to repair or replace damaged bridges without soliciting any outside help.

Working with local administration is not without challenges. However, collaboration between the local government and NGOs creates better opportunities to implement sustainable projects. Although modest in funding, the COOPI intervention in Tabarre provides a good example of a replicable project.

Summary

In this chapter, I linked the failure of the intervention to the lack of capabilities of centralized government, state corruption and the relative absence of state presence at the local level. This has resulted in conditions in which donors fund NGOs and dictate the manner in which monies have been allocated, which has produced an inherent inability of NGOs to produce long-term positive outcomes. I used a Taiwan example of disaster management in the wake of the Morakot Typhoon to demonstrate the importance of state guidance and local government involvement in disaster management. While the management of the Morakot Typhoon was done through an effective and capable state, it provided an example of what was needed for a successful rehabilitation. Then, I discussed what was lacking in the case of Haiti's post-disaster management and the problems NGOs faced in their efforts. After a discussion of the problems, I provided two examples of effective practices that could be replicated through case studies of two projects implemented by two different NGOs, which is mentioned in chapter 2. Community development may reduce vulnerabilities and increase resilience to disasters. Thus, when NGOs articulate their interventions toward community improvement, the population would benefit considerably.

Conclusion

The primary argument of this study is that disasters occur as a result of the absence of policies and practices of sustainable development that reduce vulnerabilities and build resilience. In the previous chapters, I outlined the research objectives and presented and analysed my research findings. In chapter 1, I laid out the research problem; I described the research methods and designs. In chapter 2, I addressed the conceptual and theoretical framework of the research. Three main areas of focus, which formed the backbone of my study and developed my conceptual and analytical framework, were disaster aid/relief, NGOs and development. Before I addressed the question of disaster aid, I established my theoretical perspective on disasters, which is grounded in a political economy approach. This perspective that draws heavily on the examination of disasters in the Third World views disasters as epiphenomena of broader structural, social, economic and political conditions (Blaikie 1994; Blaikie et al. 1994; Cannon 1994; Hewitt 1983–97; Hilhorst 2004; Hilhorst and Bankoff 2004–06; Lavell 1994; Oliver-Smith 2004).

Also, in chapter 2, I explored the rise of NGOs as a powerful economic force through a historical analysis. This rise coincides with the development of neoliberalism. I argued that dramatic increases in poverty in the Global South were directly tied to the effects of neoliberal policies and practices spread throughout the Third World. The rise in

NGOs is explained by the failure of both the market and central and local governments to cater to the generalized needs of the population. I examined this failure from the perspective of scholarly critiques of economic development. I employed Amartya Sen's perspective that equates development to freedom. In this regard, I added Hintzen's perspective that, while agreeing with Sen's argument, proposed that such freedom can be realized only under conditions of effective democracy and good governance. I combined these approaches with Anderson and Woodrow's understanding of development as the process by which vulnerabilities are reduced and capacities increased (Anderson and Woodrow 1998). It is this latter approach that primarily informs my book.

In chapter 3, I provided a critical analysis of the application of neoliberalism in Haiti and its social and economic implications. Haiti's reliance on NGOs is mainly a consequence of the implementation of neoliberal policies during the 1980s and 1990s. I demonstrated that these policies contributed to the weakening of the state – the condition that led to an influx of NGOs in the country.

In chapter 4, I looked at the social, economic and political conditions of Haiti. The country has been described as weak and inefficient as a result of its failure to implement policies for effective development. This has led to intense vulnerabilities among its population. I also attempt to understand "the case of Haiti" as a country with prolonged and recurrent political crises. Through the lens of Trouillot's perspective that the state has acted against the interests of the nation, I argued that the essential problem of Haiti is that the state is destroying the nation. I articulate how this conflict between the state and the nation has taken form in the decades preceding the earthquake.

In chapter 5, I described the intensity of the international community's commitments to rebuild and develop the country and argued that these commitments were not realized on the ground. Billions of dollars were channelled through NGOs for disaster relief, but the population remains even more vulnerable than before the earthquake.

Chapter 6 focused on new vulnerabilities that have been created as a consequence of the state's incapacity and reliance on NGOs. It supports a claim made in chapter 2 that even well-intentioned relief efforts may intensify pre-existing vulnerabilities and introduce new ones. In the chapter, I demonstrated that the goals that the International Donors' Conference set had not materialized in the rebuilding of Haiti; I pictured some major government buildings that have yet to be repaired or rebuilt, which can serve as an indicator of unrealized commitments. I also referred to the system and practice of public health delivery, particularly in Port-au-Prince and the construction of a new slum in Port-au-Prince as examples of exacerbated vulnerabilities in the post-earthquake period.

Chapter 7 highlights the fact that relief efforts have continued in a process I termed "unending relief". Then, I argued that for relief efforts to be successful, NGOs must incorporate development goals into aid delivery and intervention. The best way to do so is for NGOs to collaborate efficiently with local governments and organizations. I conclude the chapter with two case studies of NGO projects that underline positive practices and approaches.

In conclusion, this book informs broad debates about NGOs' capabilities to provide successful disaster relief. The case of Haiti raises doubt about the capacities of NGOs to conduct massive relief efforts in the wake of a disaster. My understanding is that while they have occasionally succeeded in this regard, they are incapable of catering to the task of rehabilitation and reconstruction. These problems are exacerbated under conditions that characterize a weak state such as Haiti, particularly given the dependence of the state on NGOs to cater to the well-being and fundamental needs of the population.

When considering the political infrastructure of international aid that favours channelling money through NGOs, I argue that for NGOs to produce positive and long-term outcomes, they need to provide aid in a manner that can build resilience to future disasters. They need to do so in ways that empower the subaltern in the communities, and they need to build resilience into their response. In this context, building disaster-resilient communities has become a centrepiece of my argument. This should also be a central part of development goals. Resilience should be built into the efforts of NGOs if they aim to deliver aid and aid relief following a disaster successfully.

The research findings allow me to critically analyse the extent to which disaster resilience was built into the post-quake NGO-provided relief in Haiti. The findings show that the Haitian population has become more vulnerable than before and, consequently, less resilient because of the failure to build resilience into their disaster intervention. This failure resulted in the incapacity of the NGOs' intervention to reinforce municipal infrastructure, restore previously existing forests and destroyed or damaged woodlands, expand tree coverage, improve access to public health, promote education and disaster awareness, contribute to gender integration and implement risk reduction practices and projects.

This is also a failure of the Haitian state. For Haiti to promote development, state actors must break with the post-colonial legacies marked by deep-seated conflicts, divisions and widespread corruption. A new nation must be reimagined with priorities of freedom, the betterment of the poor and social reconciliation between the state and the nation. Nations grow stronger when substantive freedom increases and the quality of life improves for the majority of the population.

State actors must also realign themselves and reassess their international alliances. In a time of globalization, no nation can survive in isolation. However, possibilities for human development are foreclosed when states' actors rely exclusively on the support of international actors and domestic elites whose demands conflict with the collective needs of their population. As Percy Hintzen (1989) suggests, states must seek alliances that offer the greatest freedom to shape and execute national policies that align with collective needs. Concurrently, they must reduce their dependency on resources from international actors whose interests may conflict with the broader interests of their populations. Part of the possibility of escaping from this condition largely rests upon the capacity of the national state actors to create new types of partnerships with other developing countries that can be mutually beneficial to both nations.

A fundamental contribution this book makes is that it proposes a collective strategy between NGOs and local governments to ensure better delivery of disaster aid. This is a call for devolution, a process where the local government takes the direction and ownership of their development. Devolution is a matter of public policy. It requires the central government to concede more responsibility to the local government to be able to control their development, directly negotiate with NGOs, and collaboratively implement programmes and projects as they relate to their own community needs and development goals. When authority is devolved to the local level, communities can escape the forms of disjuncture that create precarity and vulnerability operative at the national level of governance. This creates possibilities for genuine development transformation that brings with those possibilities resilience to hazards that produce disasters. The case study of COOPI in chapter 6 offers a good example of how a dynamic collaboration between the NGOs and the local government can bring about positive outcomes.

Another important finding of this study relates to community development. The study suggests community development as the best way to build resilient communities. Community development encompasses appropriate municipal infrastructure such as trash pick-up, road clearance, road construction, public housing, environmental policy, work and credit access, development of risk reduction and disaster awareness, creation of a robust public health care system and the like. The population can respond to disasters through community development to mitigate risks throughout the community. My book also includes the indicators of resilience, which are mentioned in chapter 2. Community development may reduce vulnerabilities and increase community resilience to disasters. In this way, the population would benefit considerably when NGOs articulate their interventions toward community improvement.

I advise against overgeneralizing the conclusion of this book to include developed countries. In developed countries, the states can intervene more efficiently in the wake of a disaster. In addition, in developed countries, households share risks through private insurance markets, which are willing to take risks associated with disasters. They also share risks through government-run disaster assistance programmes, which often help individuals and households affected by disasters (Dore and Etkin 2003). Besides, they usually have savings and safety nets that allow them to build even stronger capacities for recovery in the wake of a disaster. However, the results of this research may be applied to any developing country that relies on NGOs for assistance following a calamity.

Appendix: Institutional Ethnography

I investigated three NGOs (table 8.1) and conducted documentary archival research. The three NGOs – Compassion International, Cooperation International (COOPI) and GOAL Global – are working in the areas most affected by the earthquake: Port-au-Prince, Carrefour and Delmas. During this period, I participated in field activities with NGO workers, interviewed beneficiaries and visited projects on the ground. This phase was a great opportunity not only to meet people, but also to collect important documents for my research. Specifically, I collected a wealth of documents on project proposals, implementation reports, project evaluations and budgets. Compassion International is an American Christian NGO founded in 1952. According to their website, their budget is over one billion dollars, which is primarily funded through private donations and sponsorships. Because their funding sources come from private donations, they enjoy a great deal of independence in the way they manage their funds.

In contrast, COOPI and GOAL Global are younger and smaller European Organizations, with smaller budgets. COOPI is an Italian NGO and GOAL is an Irish NGO. In addition to private donations, those organizations rely enormously on funding from larger NGOs and particularly supra-international organizations like the UN. Therefore, they enjoy less autonomy in the type of programs they are implementing and how they are managing their funds.

Table 8.1: List of NGOs, Field of Intervention and Mission

NGOs	Type	Field of Intervention	Location	Mission/ Philosophy
GOAL Global	Non-religious	Infrastructure, Housing, Emergency Response and Preparedness, Resilience	Port-au-Prince	Help vulnerable communities to respond to and recover from humanitarian crises.
Compassion International	Religious	Education, Micro-finance	Carrefour, Port-au-Prince Delmas	Release children from poverty.
Cooperation International	Religious	Health, Education, Emergency Response and Preparedness Social Assistance	Port-au-Prince Delmas	Help communities in the fight against poverty, contribute to community growth, intervene in situation of emergency, reconstruction and development.

Semi-structured Interviews and Focus Groups

I conducted semi-structured interviews with top NGO directors and other relevant leaders. I interviewed international NGO consultants and high-ranking NGO officials, two of whom worked as country directors of international NGOs in Haiti. Most of my contacts with NGOs were facilitated by the Cadre de Liaison Inter-Organizations (CLIO) (Inter-Organization Liaison Framework), an association of organizations created in 2005 that tries to coordinate the activities of sixty-six Haitian and foreign organizations.

I also interviewed local NGOs and religious volunteer organizations. Particularly in the guesthouse where I stayed during my fieldwork, I met with charitable organization leaders from Canada and the United States who frequently delivered aid to Haiti post-earthquake. I interviewed mayors of different municipalities and other high-profile local and national government officials, university professors, and international charity organizations.

I conducted focus group discussions to complement the data gathered from the institutional ethnography and individual interviews. The CLIO also facilitated the contacts with the community organizations. I organized the focus groups in order to collect grassroots opinions of the NGOs' intervention after the earthquake, as well as to critically evaluate the intervention's level of success in the eyes of the community. I met with three community organizations, two of which were geared toward women – Kri Fanm Haiti (KRIFAH) and Sauve Fanm (Save the Women). The other group discussion was conducted with a very well-known community organization: *Organisation for Development et Encadrement Technique des Artisans d'Haiti* (ODSETAD) (Organization for Social Development and Technical Support of Haitian Artisans).

Household Survey

I surveyed 889 households in three cities: Port-au-Prince, Carrefour and Delmas. The objective of the survey was to measure the "perceived level of resilience" of the population and was conducted by a team of eleven individuals trained in research and data collection. The team was led by two economist-statisticians, the former head of the *Coordination Nationale de la Sécurité Alimentaire* (CNSA, or National Coordination for Food Security) in Haiti and another high-ranking consultant of the same organization.

To select the households, the survey utilized the Expanded Program on Immunization (EPI) sampling method adopted by the World Health Organization (WHO). The EPI is a cluster-sampling method that is often used to assess health and basic needs in communities affected by disasters (Malilay et al. 1996). The EPI method has been revisited and widely used in many post-disaster context surveys (Chao et al. 2012). Eighty clusters, a number based on the Primary Unit Selection (SDE) procedure established by the Haiti Institute of Statistics (HIS), were chosen with a probability proportionate to their size, and ten households were surveyed in each of the selected clusters.

Some Relevant Speeches at the International Donors' Conference on 31 March 2010

The UN Secretary Ban Ki-moon's Opening Statement:

For weeks, experts had been assessing the needs and costs of the 12 January disaster. In tandem President Préval, Prime Minister and their Government had worked out the blueprint for a national strategic plan. A plan to guide Haiti's recovery and reconstruction. He will present that vision in a moment. And I am sure you will agree that it deserves our full and generous support. As a plan for action it is concrete, specific, and above of all, ambitious.

Our goal is not just to rebuild. It is to build back better. Again, to quote the president, it is a plan to create a new Haiti, a Haiti where the majority of people no longer live in deep poverty, where they can go to school and enjoy better health, where they have better options than going without jobs or leaving the country altogether.

Under this plan, a new Interim Haiti Recovery Commission would channel $3.9 billion into specific programs and projects during the next 18 months. Over the next 10 years, Haiti's reconstruction needs will total an estimated $11.5 billion. Clearly, this assistance must be well invested and well-coordinated. In parallel with reconstruction, it must provide for continuing emergency relief, food, sanitation, health care, and most urgently, at this moment, shelter.

You are all aware how difficult is the situation right now. The rainy season is fast approaching. Some camps for displaced persons are at risk of flooding. Health and sanitation issues are growing more serious. We are also very concerned about the security situation in some of the camps, especially for women and children.

I therefore appeal for further support for the Revised Humanitarian Appeal for $1.4 billion, currently only 50% funded. As we move from emergency aid to long-term reconstruction, let us recognize that we cannot accept business as usual. What we envision today, is wholesale national renewal, a sweeping exercise in nation-building on a scale and scope not seen in generations.

The US Secretary of State Hillary Clinton's Remarks

...Some people wonder, "Why Haiti? Why this great outpouring of international humanitarian concern and commitment to Haiti's future? Why is Haiti's fate of such consequence to the region and the world that it deserves sustained help? Why should we hope that this time, with our collective assistance, Haiti can achieve a better future?" These are questions that deserve answers, and I believe that this conference will begin to do so.

There are two paths that lie before us. If Haiti can build safe homes, its citizens can escape many of the dangers they now face and return to more normal lives. If Haiti can realize broad-based, sustainable economic growth, it can create opportunity across the country beyond Port-au-Prince, so Haitians don't have to move to their capital or leave their country to find work. If Haiti can build strong health and education systems, it can give its people the tools they need to contribute to their nation's progress and fulfill their own God-given potentials. If Haiti can create strong, transparent, accountable institutions, it can establish the credibility, trust, and stability its people have long-deserved. And if Haiti can do all of those things with our help, it will become an engine for progress and prosperity generating opportunity and fostering greater stability for itself and for countries throughout the hemisphere and beyond.

But there is another path that Haiti could take, a path that demands far less of Haiti and far less of us. If the effort to rebuild is slow or insufficient, if it is marked by conflict, lack of coordination, or lack of transparency, then the challenges that have plagued Haiti for years could erupt with regional and global consequences. Before the earthquake, migration drained Haiti of many talented citizens, many of whom live in our country. If new jobs and opportunity do not emerge, even more people will leave.

Before the earthquake, hunger was a problem for Haiti. Years of deforestation had stripped the land of its rich topsoil and people struggled to grow or purchase enough food to feed their families. The riots over food that broke out in 2008 toppled Haiti's government. Now, food is even more scarce, and people more desperate.

The leaders of Haiti must take responsibility for their country's reconstruction. They must make the tough decisions that guide a strong, accountable, and transparent recovery. And that is what they are starting to do with the creation of a new mechanism that provides coordination and consultation so aid can be directed where it is most needed. And we in the global community, we must also do things differently. It will be tempting to fall back on old habits—to work around the government rather than to work with them as partners, or to fund a scattered array of well-meaning projects rather than making the deeper, long-term investments that Haiti needs now. We cannot retreat to failed strategies.

I know we've heard these imperatives before—the need to coordinate our aid, hold ourselves accountable, share our knowledge, track results. But now, we cannot just declare our intentions. We have to follow through and put them into practice. Therefore, this is not only a conference about what financially we pledge to Haiti. We also have to pledge our best efforts to do better ourselves—to offer our support in a smarter way, a more effective way that produces real results for the people of Haiti.

Notes

Preface

1. https://time.com/5609054/haiti-protests-petrocaribe/.
2. For more information about Amnesty International Index on corruption, visit their website, https://www.transparency.org/en/cpi/2018/index/hti.
3. https://time.com/5609054/haiti-protests-petrocaribe/.
4. https://plato.stanford.edu/entries/negritude/.
5. Senghor became the first president of Senegal in September 1960. He remained in office until 1980. Senghor is known not only as a major theoretician of *Négritude*, but as one of the most important African intellectuals.
6. I will spend more time in the next chapter on the characteristics of the Duvalier state.
7. 1986 corresponds to the fall of Jean Claude Duvalier and the end of a dictatorship in Haiti.

Chapter 1

1. Country Partnership Framework for the Republic of Haiti for the Period FY16–FY19.
2. Those three promoters of liberation theology are Catholic priests. The movement took root within the Catholic theologians but later extended to other non-Catholic theologians. Some of the other well-known Protestant theologians advocating for liberation theology are Rubem Alves, José Míguez Bonino and C. René Padilla.

3. The 5 July earthquake was part of a sequence of quakes that hit Southern California in July 2019. The initial shocks were followed by subsequent aftershocks. This sequence of earthquakes is mostly known as the 2019 Ridgecrest earthquakes. The initial quake shocks of magnitudes 6.4, 5.4 and 7.1 struck on 4 and 5 July. They were followed by multiple subsequent shocks. The 7.1 magnitude that occurred on 5 July is recognized as the most powerful earthquake to ever hit California since the 1999 Hector Mine earthquake, which also was a 7.1 magnitude earthquake.

4. The commune represents the third-level administrative division in Haiti. The country is divided into 10 departments. The departments are subdivided in 42 arrondissements and the latter in 144 communes. The arrondissement of Port-au-Prince, also known as the city of Port-au-Prince, is composed of 8 communes: Port-au-Prince, Carrefour, Cite Soleil, Delmas, Gressier, Kenscoff, Pétion-Ville, and Tabarre (IHSI 2015). "Mars 2015 Population Totale, Population de 18 ans et Plus Menages et Densites Estimes en 2015" (PDF). Institut Haïtien de Statistique et d'Informatique (IHSI). Archived from the original (PDF) on 6 November 2015. Retrieved 6 June 2017.

Chapter 2

1. For information about recent ODA, visit the OECD's website.

2. Zanmi Lasante (English translation for Partners in Health) began in Haiti. It was founded by the late Paul Farmer, American physician and anthropologist and the late Father Fritz Lafontant, an episcopal priest in Haiti. Partners in Health is now providing community-based health care in more than eleven countries.

3. Rostow's development approach offers a linear path for traditional societies to become developed. It presents Western societies as a "modernization" model to follow in this way as they were able to move from the initial stage of underdevelopment to advanced developed nations. The five stages of growth are: 1) Traditional society, 2) preconditions to take-off, 3) take-off, 4) drive to maturity and 5) age of high mass consumption.

4. This definition of vulnerability is from Periperi, a southern African NGO. It considers not only the socio-economic factors but the political factors that increasingly create vulnerabilities in the developing world. This definition is well suited for the case of Haiti.

Chapter 3

1. International Financial Institutions forced President Préval to initiate the privatization process. The implementation of privatization policies was an essential condition for the release of economic aid. When, under popular pressure, he decided to put the privatization process on hold, aid promised to the Haitian state was frozen. This situation continued until the end of President Préval's mandate and throughout Aristide's second term of office (1997–2004). The privatization process did not resume until March 2004, under the leadership of President Boniface Alexandre and Prime Minister Gerard Latortue, who replaced Aristide after he was ousted from power. Under Alexandre's and Latortue's leadership, the privatization process resumed under the terms of the Interim Cooperation Framework (ICF), which was signed by major donors in Haiti.

2. Marc Bazin, Government Comments (B): English version pp. 70–71. Marc Bazin was the presidential candidate that the United States supported in the 1990 elections (that eventually led Aristide's election). Marc Bazin was a former employee of the World Bank. When Aristide returned to power in 1994, the United States required that he nominate Marc Bazin as Minister of Planning and External Cooperation.

3. The Haitian government has no control of the number of NGOs in the country. Most of the NGOs are not registered. Only about five hundred NGOs are currently registered in the Ministry of Planning, the government entity in charge of regulating NGOs in the country.

4. For more information, see a distribution list of USAID funding to NGOs working in Haiti in 2007, with the type of the projects and the parallel government ministries they work with, and the amount of funding that they received (Pierre-Louis 2012, 194–95).

Chapter 4

1. The French phrase is *pays en dehors*. The peasantry was called *moun andeyo*, "people outside". It is a discriminatory way to categorize people who came from the rural areas.

2. See "Haiti and Its Occupation by the United States in 1915: Antecedents and Outcomes", published by Center for Black Studies Research.

3. The Haitian Constitution of 1987 makes the prime minister, not the president, the chief of the government. The parliament controls the government. If they are not satisfied with the performance of the government, they can give a vote of no-confidence to the prime

minister. When the prime minister receives a no-confidence vote, the government changes. A new prime minister is nominated and ratified by the parliament. The new prime minister, along with the president, will choose new cabinet members. Thus, a president may have more than one government during his term.

4. From 1986 (the year of the fall of Jean Claude Duvalier) to 1996, Haiti had known ten presidents. The period of 1997 to 2010 appeared to be more stable, with five presidents succeeded during the period. This is due to the fact that René Préval, who became president twice during this period, was able to complete both terms. As I signalled above, René Préval was the only president since the fall of Duvalier in 1996 to the date of the earthquake who concluded his term as president.

5. According to the International Crisis Group (2009), before the earthquake Haiti was on the verge of economic progress. The country was politically stable. There was also a huge relief effort to help the country following the four disasters that hit the country in 2008.

6. These figures are published in Rencoret et al. (2010). *Haiti Earthquake: Context Analysis*, 14. They are modified for the purpose of this research.

Chapter 5

1. The capital of Haiti, severely damaged by the earthquake. The National Palace is a ninety-year-old structure that was built during the American Occupation in Haiti (1915–34) (AP Photo/Tyler Anderson).

2. https://www.un.org/press/en/2010/ga10932.doc.htm.

3. https://still4hill.com/tag/haiti/.

Chapter 6

1. Professor Pierre Buteau is a former education ministry and professor at Haiti State University (P. Buteau, personal communication 2018). To protect people's identity, I have changed some names and omitted some names and identifying information. However, I keep the names of some officials and professors of the university. I had their consent to mention their names.

2. F. Dorvilier, personal communication, 2018.

3. Interview with a local NGO director.

4. Focus group with OSETAD and Save the Women.

5. The construction work of the new Haitian Parliament was started by the Dominican firm Hadom and then suspended by the government

of Haiti. It is planned to continue with the Chinese firm Hongyan Construction Company Limited (Haiti Libre 2019).

6. Interview with Professor Fritz Dorvilier.
7. We can see how people built fragile structures downhill, exposing them to the risk of possible landslide. Photo taken in August 2019 during my fieldwork in Haiti.
8. The medications used a chemical named diethylene glycol, which when contaminated is known to cause severe kidney damage. The medications were distributed by the PHARVAL SA, a pharmaceutical company in Haiti.

Chapter 7

1. Interview with a former UN consultant in Haiti.
2. GOAL is not an acronym. It is the official name of the Irish NGO. Organization's website: https://www.goalglobal.org/.
3. Interview with an official of GOAL in Haiti.
4. Interview with a CLIO's official, 2018.
5. Interview with a former UN consultant in Haiti, 2018.
6. Ibid.
7. Municipalities in Haiti are managed by a council of three mayors. The first mayor (the principal mayor) is assisted by two other mayors: (second mayor and third mayor).
8. Interview with COOPI's Head of Mission in Haiti.
9. Ibid.
10. Photo taken by Jean Max Charles during fieldwork in Haiti.
11. Some NGOs are able to work with local governments, especially on small projects. But it is more difficult for funding agencies like USAID or ECHO to work with local governments or community organizations due to legal constraints.
12. Interview with Laurent, a former UN consultant in Haiti.
13. Interview with one of the GOAL Global's foreign officials.
14. Interview with a professor of sociology at Haiti State University.
15. Interview with a professor of political economics at Haiti State University.
16. Interview with a former UN consultant in Haiti, 2018.
17. Ibid.
18. Interview with one of the Compassion International project directors.
19. Earthquake and hurricane resistant structure built by Compassion International after the earthquake. Photo taken during my fieldwork

in Haiti. According to a church leader I talked with, the structure is designated by the Haitian government as a potential public shelter in case of a natural event. And it seems to be the case for all the other school structures built by Compassion International after the earthquake.

20. Interview with COOPI's head of mission in Haiti.

References

Ahmed, Shamima, and David M. Potter. 2006. *NGOs in International Politics*. Boulder, CO: Lynne Rienner Publishers.

Allen, Katrina. 2003. "Vulnerability Reduction and Community-Based Approach: A Philippines Study." In *Natural Disasters and Development in a Globalizing World*, editing by Mark Pelling. London: Routledge.

ALNA. 2006. *Evaluating Humanitarian Action Using the OECD-DAC Criteria: An ALNAP Guide for Humanitarian Agencies*. London: Overseas Development Institute.

Anderson, Benedict. 1991. *Imagined Communities: Reflections on the Origins and the Spread of Nationalism*. 2nd ed. London: Verso.

Anderson, M. 1995. "Vulnerability to Disaster and Sustainable Development: A General Framework for Assessing Vulnerability." In Disaster Prevention for Sustainable Development, edited by C. Munasinghe. Washington, DC: World Bank.

———, and P. Woodrow. 1999. *Rising from the Ashes: Development Strategies in Times of Disasters*. London: Westview Press.

Anderson, M. B. 1996. *Do No Harm: Supporting Local Capacities for Peace Through Aid*. Cambridge, Mass.: Collaborative Effort for Development Action.

Arsht, Adrienne. 2014. "Urbanization in Latin America." *Atlantic Council*. 5 February 2014. https://www.atlanticcouncil.org/commentary/ article/urbanization-in-latin-america/#:~:text=Latin%20 America%3A%20The%20World%27s%20Urban%20 Leader&text=In%201950%2C%2040%20percent%20of,the%20 world%27s%20most%20urbanized%20region.

Arthur, Charles. 2002. *In Focus Haiti: A Guide to the People, Politics and Culture*. London: Latin America Bureau.

Bankoff, Greg. 2008. The Historical Geography of Disaster: Vulnerability and Local Knowledge. In *Mapping Vulnerability: Disasters, Development, and People*, edited by Gregg Bankoff, George Frerks and Dorothea Hilhorst. Oxford: Earthscan.

Banks, Nicola, and David Hulme. 2012. "The Role of NGOs and Civil Society in Development and Poverty Reduction." Brooks World Poverty Institute Working Paper, 1 June 2012, No. 171.

Barker, Catherine, Aaron Mulaki, and Arin Dutta. 2014. "Devolution of Healthcare in Kenya: Assessing Country Health System Readiness in Kenya: A Review of Selected Health Inputs." Health Policy Project.

Bavel, Bas Van. 2020. *Disasters and History: The Vulnerability and Resilience of Past Societies*. Cambridge: Cambridge University Press.

Bebbington, Anthony. 1997. "New States, New NGOs? Crises and Transitions among Rural Development NGOs in the Andean Region." *World Development* 25 (11): 1755–65.

———, Samuel Hickey, and Diana Mitlin. 2007. "Introduction: Can NGOs Make a Difference? The Challenge of Development Alternatives." In *Can NGOs Make a Difference? The Challenge of Development Alternatives*, edited by Anthony Bebbington, Samuel S. Hickey, and Diana Mitlin, 3–37. London: Zed Books.

Bellegarde-Smith et al. 2015. "Haiti and Its Occupation by the United States in 1915: Antecedents and Outcomes." *Journal of Haitian Studies* 21 (2): 10–43, Special Issue on the US Occupation of Haiti, 1915–34.

Black, Andrew, and Sally Evans. 1999. *Flood Damage in UK: New Insights for Insurance Industry*. Dundee: University of Dundee Press.

Blaikie, P., T. Cannon, I. Davis, and B. Wisner. 1994. *At Risk: Natural Hazards, People's Vulnerability, and Disaster*. 2nd ed. London and New York: Routledge.

Bolt, B. A. 1978. *Earthquake: A Primer*. San Francisco: W.H. Freeman.

Boothman, Dereck. 2015. *Antonio Gramsci: A Great & Terrible World – The Pre-Prison Letters, 1908–1926*. Delhi: Aakar Books.

Bossert, Thomas. 1998. "Analyzing the Decentralization of Health Systems in Developing Countries: Decision Space, Innovation and Performance." *Social Science and Medicine* 47 (10): 1513–27.

Bown, L. David, and David C. Korten. 1991. "Working More Effectively with Nongovernmental Organizations." In *Nongovernmental*

Organizations and the World Bank: Cooperation for Development, edited by Paul Samuel and Israel Arturo. Washington: World Bank.

Bradshaw, Sarah. 2014. "Engendering Development and Disasters." *Disasters* 30 (1): 19–38. London: Overseas Development Institute.

Bradshaw, S., and M. Fordham. 2013. *Women and Girls in Disasters.* Report Produced for the Department for International Development, Britain.

Breslin, Paul. 2008. The First Epic of the New World: How Shall it Be Written. In *Tree of Liberty: Cultural Legacies of the Haitian Revolution in the Atlantic World,* edited by Doris L. Garraway, 223–49. University of Virginia Press.

Brinkerhoff, D. W., and A. A. Goldsmith. 1988. "The Challenge of Administrative Reform in Post-Duvalier Haiti: Efficiency, Equity and the Prospects for Systemic Change." *International Review of Administrative Sciences,* pp. 54, 89–114.

Brunsma, David L., David Overfelt, and J. Steven Picou. 2010. *The Sociology of Katrina: Perspectives on a Modern Catastrophe.* Lanham: Rowman & Littlefield Publishers, Inc.

Buchanan-Smith, M. 1993. *A Review of OXFAM's Approach to Relief Food Distribution in Samburu and Turkana Districts of Kenya, 1992/93: The Entitlements System.* Nairobi: OXFAM.

———, and Simon Maxwell. 1994. "Linking Relief and Development: An Introduction and Overview." *IDS Bulletin* 25 (4): 2–16.

Bush, Jennifer. 1995. "The Role of Food Aid in Drought and Recovery: Oxfam's North Turkana (Kenya) Drought Relief Programme, 1992–94." *Disasters* 19 (3): 247–59.

Buttigieg, Joseph A. 1995. "Gramsci on Civil Society." *Boundary 2* 32 (3): 1–32.

Cannon, Terry. 1994. "Vulnerability Analysis and the Explanation of 'Natural Disasters.'" In *Disasters, Development, and Environment,* edited by A. Varley, 13–29. Chichester: John Wiley and Sons.

———. 2005. "The Contemporary Discourse on Civil Society: A Gramscian Critique." *Boundary 2* 32 (1): 33–52.

Carr, L.J. 1932. "Disaster and the Sequence-pattern Concept of Social Change." *American Journal of Sociology* 38, 207–18.

Cederlöf, Gustav, Donald V Kingsbury. 2019. "On PetroCaribe: Petropolitics, Energopower, and Post-Neoliberal Development in the Caribbean Energy Region." *Political Geography* 72, 124–33.

Cernea, Micheal. 1988. "Nongovernmental Organizations and Local Development." World Bank Discussion Papers, 40. Washington, DC: World Bank.

Chao, Li-Wei et al. 2012. "A Comparison of EPI Sampling, Probability Sampling, and Compact Segment Sampling Methods for Micro and Small Enterprises." *Journal of Development Economics* 98, 94–107.

Charles, Jean Max. 2002. "Psycho-sociological Analysis of Political Uprising and Violence in Haiti from (1986–1991)." Thesis presented for the Title of License in Sociology, Haiti State University.

Charles, Jean Max. 2020. "The Slave Revolt That Changed the World and the Conspiracy Against It." *Journal of Black Studies* 51 (4): 275–94.

———. 2021. "The Cost of Regime Survival: Political Instability, Underdevelopment, and (Un)natural Disasters in Haiti Before the 2010 Earthquake." *Journal of Black Studies* 52 (5): 465–81.

Chern, Jeen-Chuan, and Ching-Tsung Liu. 2014. "Morakot Post-disaster Reconstruction Management Using Public and Private Resources for Disaster Prevention and Relief Efforts." *Journal of the Chinese Institute of Engineering* 37 (5): 621–34.

Christoplos, Ian. 2003. "Actors at Risk." In Natural Disasters and Development in a Globalizing World, edited by Mark Pelling, 81–95. London: Routledge.

———. 2006. *Links Between Relief, Rehabilitation, and Development in the Tsunami Response: A Synthesis of Initial Findings.* London: Overseas Development Institute.

Crémieux, Beaulieu. 1996. *Privatisation des Entreprises d'État en Haïti: Rapport de Mission.* Montréal: Centre Canadien d'Étude et de Coopération Internationale.

Crowe, Jessica, et al. 2015. "Rural Economic Development under Devolution: A Test of Local Strategies." *Community Development* 46 (5): 461–78.

C-SPAN. 2010. "United Nations Haiti's Donors Conference." Accessed 7 June 2020. https://www.c-span.org/video/?292805-1/united-nations-haiti-donors-conference.

Davis, Ian. 2008. "Progress in Analysis of Social Vulnerability and Capacity." In *Mapping Vulnerability: Disasters, Development & the People,* edited by Greg Bankoff, Georg Frerks, and Dorothea Hilhorst, 28–44. London: Earthscan.

DAC (Development Assistance Committee). 1995. *Participatory Development and Good Governance.* Paris: OECD.

Degnbol-Martinussen, John, and Poul Engberg-Pedersen. 2005. *Aid: Understanding International Development Cooperation.* London and New York: Zed Books Ltd.

Delica-Willison, Zenaida, and Robin Willison. 2008. "Vulnerability Reduction: A Task for the Vulnerable People Themselves." In *Mapping Vulnerability: Disasters, Development & the People*, edited by Greg Bankoff, Georg Frerks, and Dorothea Hilhorst, 145–58. London: Earthscan.

Della Porta, Donatella, and Mario Diani. 2011. "Social Movements." In *The Oxford Handbook of Civil Society*, edited by Michael Edwards, 68–79. Oxford and New York: Oxford University Press.

De Meira, Luciana Fontes, and Willard Phillips. 2019. *An Economic Analysis of Flooding in the Caribbean*. Santiago: UN/ECLAC.

Desroches, Reginald, et al. 2011. "Overview of the 2010 Haiti Earthquake." *Earthquake Spectra* 27 (S1): S1–S21.

Dillon, Elizabeth Maddock, and Michael Drexler. 2016. *The Haitian Revolution and the Early United States: Histories, Textualities, Geographies*. Philadelphia: University of Pennsylvania Press.

Domar, Evsey D. 1953. "Depreciation, Replacement and Growth." *Economic Journal* 63 (249) (March): 1–32.

Dore, Mohammed H. I., and David Etkin. 2003. "Natural Disasters, Adaptive Capacity, and Development in the Twenty-first Century." In *Natural Disasters and Development in a Globalizing World*, edited by Mark Pelling, 96–112. London: Routledge.

Dorvilier, Fritz. 2018. Personal communication with the author.

Drabek, Anne Gordon. 1987. "Development Alternatives: The Challenge for NGOs: An Overview of the Issues." *World Development* 15 (1): 145–57.

Dreze, Jean, and Amartya Sen. 1989. *Hunger and Public Action*. Oxford: Clarendon Press.

Dube, Ernest. 2020. "The Build-back-better Concept as a Disaster Risk Reduction Strategy for Positive Reconstruction and Sustainable Development in Zimbabwe: A Literature Study." *International Journal of Disaster Risk Reduction*.

Duffield, Mark. 2010. "The Liberal Way of Development and the Development-Security Impasse: Exploring the Global Life-Chance Divide." *SAGE Publications* 41 (1): 53–76.

Dupuy, Alex. 1997. *Haiti in the New World Order: The Limits of the Democratic Revolution*. Boulder, CO: Westview Press.

———. 2005. "Globalization, the World Bank, and the Haitian Economy." In *Contemporary Caribbean Cultures and Societies in a Global Context*, edited by Franklin W. Knight and Teresita Martinez-Vergne, 71–93. Chapel Hill: The University of North Carolina Press.

————. 2014. *Haiti, From Revolutionary Slaves to Powerless Citizens: Essays on the Politics and Economics of Underdevelopment, 1804–1813.* London: Routledge.

Eagleton, Terry. 2013. "Introduction." In *Ideology.* London: Routledge.

ECVMAS. 2002. *Enquête sur les Conditions de Vie des Ménages Après le Séisme (Survey on the Living Conditions of Households After the Earthquake).* Port-au-Prince: IHSI.

Elbers, Willem, and B. J. M. Arts. 2011. "Keeping Body and Soul Together: Southern NGOs' Strategic Responses to Donor Constraints." *International Review of Administrative Sciences* 77 (4): 713–32.

Embassy of the Republic of Haiti in Washington, DC (ERHW). n.d. "Haiti at a Glance." Accessed 6 June 2020. https://www.haiti.org/haiti-at-a-glance/.

EM-DAT. The OFDA/CRED International Disaster Database. Université catholique de Louvain–Brussels–Belgium. http://www.emdat.be. Retrieved in 2018.

Escobar, Arturo. 1995. *Encountering Development: The Making and Unmaking of the Third World.* Princeton: Princeton University Press.

————. 1997. "The Making and Unmaking of the Third World." In *The Post Development Reader*, edited by Majid Rahnema and Victoria Bawtree, 85–93. London: Zed Books.

Etienne, Hadlaire. 2010. "Dilemmes et Enjeux des Privatisations des Entreprises Publiques pour l'Etat Haitien." Master's thesis, Quebec University at Montreal.

Etienne, Sauveur Pierre. 1997. *Haiti: L'Invasion des ONGs.* Montreal: Les Editions CIDIHCA.

Farmer, Paul. 2006. *The Uses of Haiti.* 3rd ed. Monroe, ME: Common Courage Press.

Fatton, Robert. 2007. *The Roots of Haitian Despotism.* Boulder, CO: Lynne Rienner Publishers.

Fatton, Robert Jr. 2002. *Haiti's Predatory Republic: The Unending Transition to Democracy.* Chapel Hill: University of North Carolina Press.

————. 2013. "Michel-Rolph Trouillot's State Against Nation: A Critique of the Totalitarian Paradigm." *Small Axe* 42:78–92.

Ferguson, James. 1987. *Papa Doc, Baby Doc: Haiti and the Duvaliers.* Oxford: Basil Blackwell Ltd.

————. 1999. "Haiti: Country Profile." *The New Internationalist.* Accessed 28 March 2020. https://newint.org/features/1999/09/05/profile#:~:text=It%20has%20more%20millionaires%20per,per%20person%20of%20around%20%24250.

————. 2006. *Global Shadows: Africa in the Neoliberal World Order*. Durham: Duke University Press.

Escobar, Arturo (1995). *Encountering Development: The Making and Unmaking of the Third World*. Princeton University Press.

Fils-Aimé, Romaric. 2018. "PHARVAL S.A. et plus de 200 enfants morts: Qu'en est-il 22 ans après?" AyiboPost. Accessed 28 March 2020. https://ayibopost.com/pharval-s-a-et-plus-de-200-enfants-morts-quen-est-il-22-ans-apres.

Fisher, Henry W. 1998. *Response to Disaster, Fact Versus Fiction: The Sociology of Disaster*. Lanham, MD: University Press of America.

Fritz, Charles. 1961. "Disasters." In *Contemporary Social Problems*, edited by Robert K. Merton and Robert A. Nisbet, 651–94. New York: Harcourt.

Galway, Lindsay P., Kitty K. Corbett, and Leilei Zeng. 2012. "Where Are the NGOs and Why? The Distribution of Health and Development NGOs in Bolivia." *Globalization and Health* 8 (38). https://globalizationandhealth.biomedcentral.com/articles/10.1186/1744-8603-8-38#:~:text=NGO%20activity%20tends%20to%20be,among%20NGOs%20working%20in%20Bolivia.

GOH (Government of Haiti). 2010. *Haïti PDNA du Tremblement de Terre—Evaluation des Dommages, des Pertes et des Besoins Généraux et Sectoriels: Annexe du Plan d'Action pour le Relèvement et le Développement National d'Haïti*. Port-au-Prince: Government of Haiti.

Goldin, Ian. 2016. *The Pursuit of Development: Economic Growth, Social Change, and Ideas*. Oxford: Oxford University Press.

Grenier, Guillermo J., and Betty H. Morrow. 1997. "Before the Storm: The Socio-Political Ecology of Miami." In *Hurricane Andrew: Ethnicity, Gender, and the Sociology of Disasters*, edited by Gillis W. Peacock, Betty H. Morrow, and Hugh Gladwin, 50–71. London and New York: Routledge.

Grove, Kevin. 2013. "Insuring 'Our Common Future': Dangerous Climate Change and the Biopolitics of Environmental Security." *Geopolitics* 15:536–63.

————. 2013. "Hidden Transcripts of Resilience: Power and Politics Jamaican Disaster Management." *Resilience* 1 (3): 193–209.

————. 2014. "Agency, Affect, and the Immunological Politics of Disaster Resilience." *Environment and Planning D: Society and Space* 32: 240–56.

Grünewald, F., and B. Renaudin. 2010. *Etude en Temps Réel de la Gestion de la Crise en Haïti Après le Séisme du 12 Janvier 2010: Mission du 9 au 23 février 2010.* Mission Report, Delegation of Strategic Affairs of the Ministry of Defense, Republic of France, 14 April.

Guha-Sapir, D., et al. 2012. *Annual Disaster Statistical Review 2011: The Numbers and Trends.* Brussels: CRED.

Gustafson, E. 1998. "Gender Differences in Risk Perception: Theoretical and Methodological Perspectives." *Risk Analysis* 18 (6): 805–11.

Haddon, W., E. A. Suchman, and D. Klein. 1964. *Accident Research: Methods and Approaches.* New York: Harper & Row.

Haiti Libre. 2013. "Haiti – Economy: The Amount of Remittances in Haiti has Doubled in 10 Years." *Haiti Libre,* 30 April 2013. https://www.haitilibre.com/en/news-8459-haiti-economy-the-amount-of-remittances-in-haiti-has-doubled-in-10-years.html.

———. 2015. "Haiti – Politique: 5 Nouvelles Communes en Haiti." *Haiti Libre,* 16 August 2015. https://www.haitilibre.com/en/news-14858-haiti-politic-5-new-communes-in-haiti.html.

Haiti Info. 1995. "Privatization: What the Haitian People Can Expect?" *Haiti Info* 3 (10).

Haiti Observer. 2013. "Michèle Bennett, Former First Lady of Haiti and the Ex-wife of Jean-Claude Duvalier." http://www.haitiobserver.com/blog/tag/first-lady/michele-bennett-former-first-lady-of-haiti-and-the-ex-wife-o.html.

Hallward, Peter. 2007. Damming the Flood: Haiti, Aristide and the Politics of Containment. London: Verso.

Harrod, Royd. 1973. *Economic Dynamics.* London: Macmillan.

Heinl, R. D., and N. G. Heinl. 2005. *Written in the Blood: The Story of the Haitian People, 1492–1995.* Lanham, MD: University Press of America.

Hejimans, Annelies. 2008. "From Vulnerability to Empowerment." In *Mapping Vulnerability: Disasters, Development & the People,* edited by Greg Bankoff, Georg Frerks, and Dorothea Hilhorst, 161–77. London: Earthscan.

Hejimans, A., and L. Victoria. 2001. *Citizenry-Based and Development-Oriented Disaster Response: Experience and Practice in Disaster Management of the Citizen Disaster Response Network in Philippines.* Manila: Center for Disaster Preparedness.

Henderson, J.V., and Y.S. Lee. 2015. "Organization of Disaster Aid Delivery: Spending Your Donations." *Economic Development and Cultural Change* 63 (4): 617–64.

Hewitt, K. 1983. *Interpretations of Calamities from the Viewpoints of Human Ecology*. London: Allen and Unwin Inc.

———. 1995. "Sustainable Disasters? Perspectives and Power in the Discourse of Calamity." In *Power and Development*, edited by J. Crush, 115–28. London and New York: Routledge.

———. 1997. *Regions at Risk: A Geographical Introduction to Disasters*. London: Routledge.

Heywood, Andrew. 1994. *Political Ideas: An Introduction*. London: Macmillan.

Hilhorst, Dorothea. 2004. "Complexity and Diversity: Unlocking Social Domains of Disaster Response." In *Mapping Vulnerability: Disasters, Development & People*, edited by Greg Bankoff, Georg Frerks, and Dorothea Hilhorst, 55–69. London: Earthscan.

———, and Greg Bankoff. 2004. "Theorizing Vulnerability in a Globalized World: A Political Ecology Perspective." In *Mapping Vulnerability: Disasters, Development & People*, edited by Greg Bankoff, Georg Frerks, and Dorothea Hilhorst. London: Earthscan.

Hintzen, Percy. 1989. *The Cost of Regime Survival: Racial Mobilization, Elite Domination, and the Control of the State in Guyana and Trinidad*. Cambridge: Cambridge University Press.

———. 1995. "Structural Adjustment and the New International Middle-Class." *Transition* 24: 53–73.

———. 2014. "After Modernization: Globalization and the African Dilemma." In *Modernization as Spectacle in Africa*, edited by Peter J. Bloom, Takyiwaa Manuh, and Stephan Miescher, 2–39. Bloomington: Indiana University Press.

———. 2018a. "Rethinking Identity, National Sovereignty, and the State: Reviewing Some Critical Contributions." *Social Identities* 24 (1): 39–47.

———. 2018b. "Towards a New Democracy in the Caribbean: Local Empowerment and the New Global Order." In *Beyond Westminster in the Caribbean*, edited by Brian Meeks and Kate Quinn. Kingston: Ian Randle Publishers.

———. 2019. "Precarity and the HIV/AIDS Pandemic in the Caribbean: Structural Stigma, Constitutionality, Legality in Development Practice." Global Public Health.

Huntington, Ellsworth. 1945. *Mainsprings of Civilizations*. New York: Wiley.

IFRC (International Federation of Red Cross and Red Crescent Societies). 2019. Country Acceleration Plan 2019 – Haiti. Accessed 27 July 2024. https://reliefweb.int/report/haiti/ifrc.

International Crisis Group. 2009. Haiti 2009: Stability at Risk. Latin America and Caribbean Briefing No. 19. Port-au-Prince/Brussels.

———, and Greg Bankoff, Greg. 2004. "Theorizing Vulnerability in a Globalized World: A Political Ecology Perspective." In *Mapping Vulnerability: Disasters, Development & People*, edited Bankoff, Greg, Frerks Geog, Hilhorst Dorothea. London: Earthscan.

IPCC, 2023: "Summary for Policymakers." In *Climate Change 2023: Synthesis Report. Contribution of Working Groups I, II and III to the Sixth Assessment Report of the Intergovernmental Panel on Climate Change* [Core Writing Team, H. Lee and J. Romero (eds.)]. IPCC, Geneva, Switzerland, 1–34, doi: 10.59327/IPCC/AR6-9789291691647.001

ISDR (International Strategy for Disaster Reduction). 2004. *Living with Risk: A Global Review of Disaster Reduction Initiatives*. Geneva: UN Publications.

———. 2005. Hyogo Framework for Action 2005–2015: "Building the Resilience of Nations and Communities." World Conference on Disaster Reduction, 18–22 January, Kobe, Hyogo, Japan.

Janse, Harmen, and Kees V. D. Flier. 2014. "Cordaid's Post Disaster Shelter Strategy in Haiti: Linking Relief and Development." *Open House International* 39 (3): 30–40.

Jean-Baptiste, Christine. 2021. "Racist Stereotypes About Haiti in the Media Dehumanize Haitians." *Teen Vogue*. 18 March 2021. https://www.teenvogue.com/story/racist-stereotypes-haiti-media.

Kaldor, Mary. 2008. *Global Civil Society: An Answer to War*. Cambridge: Polity Press.

Kaplan, Sarah, Rong-Gong Lin II, and Jaclyn Cosgrove. 2019. "Second Stronger Quake in Ridgecrest Shakes Southern California, Causing More Damage." *Los Angeles Times*, 5 July 2019.

Keck, Margaret, and Kathryn Sikkink. 1998. *Activists beyond Borders*. Ithaca, NY: Cornell University Press.

Kirton, Mark. 2013. *Caribbean Regional Disaster Response and Management Mechanism: Prospects and Challenges*. Washington, DC: Brookings Institution.

Klarreich, Kathie, and Linda Polman. 2012. "The NGO Republic of Haiti." *The Nation*, 19 November 2012. https://www.thenation.com/article/archive/ngo-republic-haiti/.

Knauer, Kelly. 2012. *Time: Disasters That Shook the World*. London: International ISBN Agency.

Kreutzmann, Hermann, and Sophia Schütte. 2011. "Linking Relief and Development in Pakistan-Administered Kashmir." *Mountain Research and Development* 31 (2): 122–31.

Kuhn, Thomas S. 1962. *The Structure of Scientific Knowledge.* Chicago: University of Chicago Press.

Kuznets, Simon. 1971. *Economic Growth of Nations: Total Output and Production Structure.* Cambridge: Belknap Press of Harvard University Press.

———. 1973. *Population, Capital, and Growth: Selected Essays.* New York: W. W. Norton & Co.

Landman, Todd, and Meghna Abraham. 2004. *Evaluation of Nine Human Rights Organizations.* The Hague: Ministry of Foreign Affairs.

Lavell, Allan. 1994. "Prevention and Mitigation of Disasters in Central America: Vulnerability to Disasters at a Local Level." In *Disasters, Development, and Environment,* edited by Ann Varley, 133–59. Manchester: Wiley.

Lebrun, Marc-Evens. 2019. "Pharmacie Ambulante, un Risque Majeur de Santé Publique en Haïti." *Loop,* 25 July 2018. https://haiti.loopnews.com/content/la-vente-des-medicaments-ambulants-un-risque-majeur-de-sante-publique.

Le Nouvelliste. 2009. "Les Moulins d'Haïti: Première Entreprise Recensée."

———. 2015. "Un Recensement Dénombre Plus de 70 000 Agents dans la Fonction Publique Haïtienne."

Leibenstein, Harvey. 1957. *Economic Backwardness and Economic Growth.* New York: Wiley.

Lewis, David. 2002. "Civil Society in African Contexts: Reflections on the Usefulness of a Concept." *Development and Change* 33 (4): 569–86.

———. Sustainability." *The Annals of the American Academy of Political and Social Science* 590:212–26.

———, Nazneen Kanji, and Nuno S. Themudo. 2021. *Non-Governmental Organizations and Development.* 2nd ed. London: Routledge.

Lizarralde, Gonzalo, et al. 2004. "A System Approach to Resilience in the Built Environment: The Case of Cuba." *Overseas Development Institute* 39 (SI): S76–S95.

Lizarralde, Gonzalo. 2002. "Organisational Design, Performance, and Evaluation of Post-Disaster Reconstruction Projects." *ResearchGate.* https://www.researchgate.net/publication/239611877_ORGANISATIONAL_DESIGN_PERFORMANCE_AND_EVALUATION_OF_POST-DISASTER_RECONSTRUCTION_PROJECTS.

————. 2021. *Unnatural Disasters: Why Most Responses to Risk and Climate Change Fail but Some Succeed*. New York: Columbia University Press.

Maguire, Robert. 2008. "Review of *The Roots of Haitian Despotism*, by Robert Fatton." *Journal of Haitian Studies* 14 (1): 238–40.

Malilay, Joseph, Donna Brogan, and W. D. Flanders. 1996. "A Modified Cluster-Sampling Method for Post-Disaster Rapid Assessment of Needs." *Bulletin of the World Health Organization* 74 (4): 399–405.

Martinussen, John D., and Poul E. Pedersen. 2005. *Understanding International Development Cooperation*. London: Zed Books.

Mbembe, Achille. 2017. *Critique of Black Reason*. Durham: Duke University Press.

McElroy, Ann, and Patricia K. Townsend. 2015. *Medical Anthropology in Ecological Perspective*. 6th ed. London: Taylor & Francis Group.

McFadden, David. 2017. "Haiti to Rebuild National Palace Smashed in 2010 Earthquake." *AP News*, 19 April 2017.

McMichael, Philip. 2012. *Development and Social Change: A Global Perspective*. London: Sage.

Meehan, Kevin. 2004. "Review of *Haiti's Predatory Republic: The Unending Transition to Democracy* by Robert Fatton, Jr." *Latin Americanist* 48 (1): 92–95.

Meyer-Joassaint, Nadège. 2020. *La Protection du Droit au Logement dans la Législation Haitienne au Regard des Normes Internationales*. Quebec City: Université Laval.

Microtrends. 2020. "Port-au-Prince, Haiti Metro Area Population 1950–2020." Accessed 7 June 2020. https://www.macrotrends.net/cities/21133/port-au-prince/population.

Mitlin, Diana, et al. 2005. "Reclaiming Development? NGOs and the Challenges of Alternatives." Background paper for the Third Manchester Conference on NGOs.

Moral, Paul. 1961. *Le Paysan Haitien: Etude sur la Vie Rurale en Haiti*. Port-au-Prince: Ed. Fardin.

Mosel, Irina, and Simon Levine. 2014. *Remaking the Case for Linking Relief, Rehabilitation and Development*. Berlin: Federal Ministry for Economic Cooperation and Development.

Mother Earth Travel. 2020. "Haiti Population." Accessed 7 June 2020. http://motherearthtravel.com/haiti/population.htm.

Nurkes, R. 1953. *Problems of Capital Formation in Under-Developed Countries*. Oxford: Oxford University Press.

Nwankwo, Ifeao C. K. 2008. "'Charge with Sympathy for Haiti': Harshening the Power of Blackness and Cosmopolitanism in the Wake of the Haitian Revolution." In *Tree of Liberty: Cultural Legacies of the Haitian Revolution*, edited by Doris L. Garraway, 91–113. Charlottesville: University of Virginia Press.

Oakley, Peter, and Susan Floke. 1999. *The Danish NGOs Impact Study: A Review of Danish NGOs Activities in Developing Countries. Synthesis Report.* Copenhagen: Danida, Ministry of Foreign Affairs.

O'Byrne, Darren. 2013. "Dealing with Disasters in an Age of Globalized Sentiment: Testing the Boundaries of the Cosmopolitan Ideal?" *Perspectives on Global Development and Technology* 12 (1–2): 283–97.

OECD (Organization for Economic Cooperation and Development). 1988. *Voluntary Aid for Development: The Role of Non-Governmental Organizations.* Paris: OECD.

———. 2004. *Assessment Framework for Coverage of Humanitarian Action in Peer Review.* Paris: OECD.

Oliver-Smith, Anthony. 2004. "Theorizing Vulnerability: A Political Ecological Perspective." In *Mapping Vulnerability: Disasters, Development, & the People*, edited by Greg Bankoff, Georg Frerks, and Dorothea Hilhorst. London: Earthscan.

———, and Susanna M. Hoffman. 2001. "Theorizing Disasters: Nature, Power, and Culture." In *Catastrophe and Culture: The Anthropology of Disasters*, edited by Susanna M. Hoffman and Anthony Oliver-Smith. Santa Fe: School of American Research Press.

Olivier, Louis-Joseph. 2015. "Creation de Cinq Nouvelles Communes par Decret Presidentiel." *Le Nouvelliste*, 14 August 2015.

Olopade, Dayo. 2014. *The Bright Continent: Breaking Rules and Making Change in Modern Africa.* Boston: Houghton Mifflin Harcourt.

O'Loughlin, Karen F., and James F. Lander. 2003. *Caribbean Tsunamis: A 500-Year History from 1498–1998.* Dordrecht: Springer Science.

Ong, Aihwa. 1999. *Flexible Citizenship: The Cultural Logics of Transnationality.* Durham, NC: Duke University Press.

OSGSA (Office of the Special Representative for the Secretary-General for Haiti). 2010. "Interim Haiti Recovery Mission: Background Information." 17 June 2020. http://www.lessonsfromhaiti.org/lessons-from-haiti/interim-haiti-recovery-commission/.

Otto, Ralf, and Ludwig Weingärtner. 2013. "Linking Relief and Development: More Than Old Solutions for Old Problems?" Channel Research on Behalf of the Dutch Ministry of Foreign Affairs, IOB.

Ozerdem, Alpaslan. 2003. "Manifestation of Unresolved Development Challenges." In *Natural Disasters and Development in a Globalizing World*, edited by Mark Pelling. London: Routledge.

Pancap. 2017. "HIV and AIDS in the Caribbean." https://pancap.org/pancap-documents/hiv-and-aids-in-the-caribbean-2/.

Passport Health. 2015. "What Do I Need to Know About Cholera in Haiti?" Accessed 7 June 2020. https://www.passporthealthusa.com/2015/05/cholera-outbreak-in-haiti-protect-yourself/.

Peet, Richard, and Elaine Hartwick. 2009. *Theories of Development: Contentions, Arguments, Alternatives*. New York: The Guilford Press.

Perry, Ronald W. 2006. "What Is a Disaster?" In *Handbook of Disaster Research*, edited by Havidán Rodríguez, Enrico L. Quarantelli, and Russell R. Dynes. New York: Springer.

Pierre-Charles, Gérard. 1973. *Radiographie d'une Dictature: Haiti et Duvalier*. Montreal: Nouvelle Optique.

Pierre-Louis, Francois. 2011. "Earthquakes, Nongovernmental Organizations, and Governance in Haiti." *Journal of Black Studies* 42 (2): 186–202.

Polanyi, Karl. 1957. *The Great Transformation: The Political and Economic Origins of Our Time*. Boston: Beacon Press.

Prasad, Abhaya, and Louis H. Francescutti. 2017. "Natural Disasters." In *International Encyclopedia of Public Health*, 2nd ed., vol. 5, 215–22.

Quarantelli, E. L. 1985. "What Is a Disaster? The Need for Clarification and Conceptualization in Research." In *Disasters and Mental Health: Selected Contemporary Perspectives*, edited by Solomon S., 41–73. Washington, DC: US Government Printing Office.

———. 1991. "More and Worse Disasters in the Future." Paper presented at the UCLA International Conference on the Impact of Natural Disasters: Agenda for Future Action, Los Angeles, California, 10–12 July.

———. 2002. "The Disaster Research Center (DRC) Field Studies of Organized Behavior in Disasters." In *Methods of Disaster Research*, edited by Robert Stallings, 94–116. Philadelphia: Xlibris.

Rahnema, Majid, and Victoria Bawtree, eds. 1997. *The Post Development Reader*. London: Zed Books.

Ramachandran, Vijaya, and Julie Walz. 2015. "Haiti: Where Has All the Money Gone?" *Journal of Haitian Studies* 21 (1): 26–65.

Ramet, Valerie. 2012. "Linking Relief, Rehabilitation and Development: Towards More Effective Aid." European Union Parliament, Policy Briefing.

Reid, Julian. 2012. "The Neoliberal Subject: Resilience and the Art of Living Dangerously." In *Resilience: The Governance of Complexity*, edited by David Chandler and Julian Reid, 143–65. Chichester: Wiley.

Reimann, Kim D. 2006. "A View from the Top: International Politics, Norms and the Worldwide Growth of NGOs." Political Science Faculty Publications.

Reinhardt, Thomas. 2005. "200 Years of Forgetting: Hushing up the Haitian Revolution." *Journal of Black Studies* 35 (4): 246–61.

Rencoret, Nicole. 2006. "Evaluating Humanitarian Action Using the OECD-DAC Criteria." *ALNAP*, 1 March 2006. https://alnap. org/humanitarian-resources/publications-and-multimedia/ evaluating-humanitarian-action-using-the-oecd-dac-criteria/.

————, et al. 2010. Haiti Earthquake Response: Country Analysis. ALNAP.

Reno, William. 1999. *Warlord Politics and African States*. Boulder, CO: Lynne Rienner Publishers.

Riddell, Roger C. 2008. *Does Foreign Aid Really Work?* Oxford: Oxford University Press.

Riddell, Roger, et al. 1997. *Searching for Impact and Methods: NGO Evaluation Synthesis Study*, vol. 2. Helsinki: Department for International Development Cooperation, Ministries for Foreign Affairs of Finland.

Robert, Arnaud. 2017. "The Side Effect." *National Geographic*.

Ross, J., Simon Maxwell, and Margaret Buchanan-Smith. 1994. "Linking Relief and Development." *Institute of Development Studies*. https:// www.ids.ac.uk/download.php?file=files/dmfile/DP344.pdf.

Rostow, Walt W. 1960. *The Stages of Economic Growth: A Non-Communist Manifesto*. Cambridge: Cambridge University Press.

Ruffman, Alan, and Colin D. Howell, eds. 1994. *Ground Zero: A Reassessment of the 1917 Explosion in Halifax Harbour*. Halifax: Nimbus Publishing.

Sajinés, Javier. 2007. "The Nation: An Imagined Community." *Cultural Studies* 21 (2–3): 295–308.

Salamon, Lester M. 1994. "The Rise of the Non-Profit Sector." *Foreign Affairs* 73 (4): 109–22.

Salt, Julian E. 2003. "The Insurance Industry: Can It Cope with Catastrophe?" In *Natural Disasters and Development in a Globalizing World*, edited by Mark Pelling, 68–88. London: Routledge.

Scherer, J. 1912. "Great Earthquakes in the Island of Haiti." *Bulletin of the Seismological Society of America* 2 (3): 161–80.

Schiller, Nina Glick, and Georges Fouron. 2001. *Georges Wake Up Laughing: Long-Distance Nationalism and the Search for Home.* Durham, NC: Duke University Press.

Schipper, Lisa, and Mark Pelling. 2006. "Disaster Risk, Climate Change and International Development: Scope for, and Challenges to, Integration." *Disasters* 30 (1): 19–38.

Schuller, Mark. 2007. "Invasion or Infusion? Understanding the Role of NGOs in Contemporary Haiti." *Journal of Haitian Studies* 13 (2): 96–111.

———. 2009. "Gluing Globalization: NGOs as Intermediaries in Haiti." *Political and Legal Anthropology Review* 32 (1): 84–104.

———. 2012. *Killing with Kindness: Haiti, International Aid, and NGOs.* New Brunswick, NJ: Rutgers University Press.

Sen, Amartya. 1981. *Poverty and Famines: An Essay on Entitlement and Deprivation.* Oxford: Oxford University Press.

———. 1999. *Development as Freedom.* New York: Anchor Books.

Shigetomi, Shinichi. 2002. *The State and the NGOs: Perspective from Asia.* Singapore: Institute of Southeast Asian Studies.

Singh, Rabin, and Mary Barton-Dock. 2015. *Haiti: Toward a New Narrative.* Washington, DC: World Bank Group.

Sirleaf, Ellen Johnson. 1993. "From Disaster to Development." In *A Framework for Survival: Health, Human Rights and Humanitarian Assistance in Conflicts and Disasters,* edited by Kevin Cahill, 71–90. New York: Basic Books and the Council of Foreign Relations.

Smith, Brian. 1998. "Nonprofit Organizations in International Development: Agents of Empowerment or Preservers of Stability." In *Private Action and the Public Good,* edited by Walter W. Powell and Elisabeth Clemens, 212–27. New Haven, CT: Yale University Press.

Smith, Bronte. 2013. *The Role of Vegetation in Catastrophic Floods: A Spatial Analysis.* Wollongong: University of Wollongong.

Solovieve, S. L. 1978. "Tsunamis." In *UNESCO,* 118–139.

Solow, Robert. 1956. "A Contribution to the Theory of Economic Growth." *Quarterly Journal of Economics* 70 (1): 65–94.

Sternberg, Elaine. 2010. "NGOs vs Civil Society: Reflections on the Illiberal, the Illegitimate, and the Unaccountable." *Economic Affairs* 30 (4): 22–28.

Stiles, Kendall W. 1998. "Civil Society Empowerment and Multilateral Donors: International Institutions and New International Norms." *Global Governance* 4:199–216.

———. 2002. "International Support for NGOs in Bangladesh: Some Unintended Consequences." *World Development* 30 (5): 835–46.

Strauss, Anselm, and Juliet Corbin. 1998. *Basics of Qualitative Research: Techniques and Procedures for Developing Grounded Theory.* Thousand Oaks, CA: Sage Publications, Inc.

Strudsholm, Tina. 2016. "Using Mixed Methods to Facilitate Complex, Multiphased Health Research." *International Journal of Qualitative Methods* 15 (1): 1–8.

Tarp, Finn. 2000. *Foreign Aid and Development: Lessons Learnt and Directions for the Future.* New York: Routledge.

Thompson, Chris, and Jacky Croke. 2013. "Geomorphic Effects, Flood Power, and Channel Competence of a Catastrophic Flood in Confined and Unconfined Reaches of the Upper Lockyer Valley, Southeast Queensland, Australia." *ResearchGate.* https://www. researchgate.net/publication/260724682_Geomorphic_effects_ flood_power_and_channel_competence_of_a_catastrophic_ flood_in_confined_and_unconfined_reaches_of_the_upper_ Lockyer_valley_southeast_Queensland_Australia.

Thorbecke, Erik. 2006. *The Evolution of the Development Doctrine and the Role of Foreign Aid.* Tokyo: United Nations University.

Toblin, J. 1977. "Disaster Prevention and Control in Earth Sciences." *Impact of Science on Society* 27:131–39.

Todoroki, Emiko, Matteo Vaccani, and Wameek Noor. 2009. *The Canada-Caribbean Remittance Corridor: Fostering Formal Remittances to Haiti and Jamaica through Effective Regulation.* Washington, DC: The World Bank.

Torpey-Saboe, Nichole. 2015. "Does NGO Presence Decrease Government Spending? A Look at Municipal Spending on Social Services in Brazil." *World Development* 74:479–88.

Townsend, Janet G., Gina Porter, and Emma Mawdsley. 2004. "Creating Spaces of Resistance: Development NGOs and Their Clients in Ghana, India, and Mexico." *Antipode* 36 (5): 871–89.

Trouillot, Michel R. 2000. *Haiti: State Against Nation: Origins and Legacy of Duvalierism.* New York: Monthly Review Press.

———. 2001. "The Anthropology of the State in the Age of Globalization: Close Encounters of the Deceptive Kind." *Current Anthropology* 42 (1): 125–38.

Twigg, John. 2009. *Characteristics of a Disaster-Resilient Community.* London: Latitude Graphic Design.

Ulysse, Gina Athena. 2015. *Why Haiti Needs New Narratives: A Post-Quake Chronicle.* Middletown, CT: Wesleyan University Press.

UNDP (United Nations Development Programme). 2015. "A Cuban Model for a Resilient Caribbean." Accessed July 27, 2024. https://www.undp.org/%20Cuban%20model%20for%20a%20resilient%20Caribbean%20_%20UNDP.htm.

———. 2019. *Inequalities in Human Development in the 21st Century: Briefing Note for Countries on the 2019 Human Development Report (Haiti)*. New York: UNDP.

United Nations. 1987. *Our Common Future: Report of the World Commission on Environment and Development*. New York: United Nations.

———. 2002. *Johannesburg Declaration on Sustainable Development*. New York: United Nations.

———. 2004. *Living with Risk: A Global Review of Disaster Reduction Initiatives*. Geneva: International Strategy for Disaster Reduction (ISDR).

———. 2005. *Investing in Development: A Practical Plan to Achieve the Millennium Development Goals*. London: Earthscan.

———. 2010. "Towards a New Future for Haiti." *UN Chronicle*.

———. 2017. *Report of the Secretary-General on the United Nations Stabilization Mission in Haiti*. United Nations Security Council.

United Nations Department of Economic and Social Affairs, Statistical Office. 1976. "Population of Capital and Cities of 100,000 and More Inhabitants." In *Demographic Yearbook 1975*, 253–79. New York: United Nations.

United States Department of Commerce. 2019. "Haiti – Travel and Tourism." Accessed February 14, 2019. https://www.export.gov/article?id=Haiti-Travel-and-Tourism.

Van der Maren, Jean-Marie. 1995. *Méthodes de recherche pour l'éducation*. Montréal: Les Presses de l'Université de Montréal.

Verner, Dorte. 2007. "The Haitian People: Demographics, Poverty, and Socioeconomic Outcomes and Risks." *In Social Resilience and State Fragility in Haiti*, 45–78. Washington, DC: The World Bank.

Ward, Patrick S., and Gerald E. Shively. 2017. "Disaster Risk, Social Vulnerability, and Economic Development." *Disasters* 41 (4): 697–720.

West, Madeline. 2014. "Community Water and Sanitation Alternatives in Peri-Urban Cochabamba: Progressive Politics or Neoliberal Utopia?" Master's thesis, University of Ottawa, School of International Development Studies, Faculty of Social Sciences.

White, Gilbert F. 1945. *Human Adjustment to Floods: A Geographical Approach to the Flood Problem in the United States*. Chicago: University of Chicago Press.

White, Sarah C. 1999. "NGOs, Civil Society, and the State in Bangladesh: The Politics of Representing the Poor." *Development and Change* 30 (2): 307–26.

Wilentz, Amy. 2019. "The Other Notre-Dame Was Not Rebuilt: Perhaps France Should Help Haiti, Its Former Colony, Rebuild the Cathedral Lost in the 2010 Earthquake." *The Atlantic*, 28 April 2019.

Willett, Joanie. 2016. "Cornwall's Devolution Deal: Towards a More Sustainable Governance." *Political Quarterly* 87 (4): 582–89.

Willetts, Peter. 2011. *Non-Governmental Organizations in World Politics: The Construction of Global Governance*. London: Routledge.

Wilson Center. 2023. "Two Years After Moïse Assassination: The Impact of Gang Violence in Haiti." 13 September 2023. https://www.wilsoncenter.org/event/two-years-after-moise-assassination-impact-gang-violence-haiti.

Wisner, Ben. 1993. "Disaster Vulnerability: Scale, Power, and Daily Life." *GeoJournal* 30 (2): 127–40.

———. 1996. "The Geography of Vulnerability." In *Preparing for the Big One in Tokyo: Urban Earthquake Risk Management*, edited by J. Uitto and J. Schneider, 115–32. Tokyo: United Nations University.

———. 1998. "The Geography of Vulnerability: Why the Tokyo Homeless Don't 'Count' in Earthquake Preparation." *Applied Geography* 18 (1): 25–34.

———. 2008. "Assessment of Capability and Vulnerability." In *Mapping Vulnerability: Disasters, Development & the People*, edited by Greg Bankoff, Georg Frerks, and Dorothea Hilhorst, 183–202. London: Earthscan.

World Bank. 1995. *Working with NGOs: A Practical Guide to Operational Collaboration between the World Bank and Non-Governmental Organizations*. Washington, DC: Operations Policy Department, 7–9.

———. 1996. *Country Assistance Strategy of the World Bank Group for the Republic of Haiti*. Washington, DC: The World Bank Group.

———. 1998. *Haiti: The Challenge of Poverty Reduction. Report No. 17242-HA*. Washington, DC: The World Bank.

———. 2002. *Haiti: Country Assistance Evaluation*. Washington, DC: Operations Evaluation Department, The World Bank.

———. 2003. *Poverty and Climate Change: Reducing the Vulnerability of the Poor through Adaptation*. Washington, DC: The World Bank.

———. 2005. *HIV/AIDS in the Caribbean Region: A Multi-Organization Review*. Washington, DC: The World Bank.

———. 2007. *The Haitian People: Demographics, Poverty, and Socioeconomic Outcomes and Risks in Social Resilience.* Washington, DC: The World Bank.

———. 2017. "Rapidly Assessing the Impact of Hurricane Matthew in Haiti." https://www.worldbank.org/en/results/2017/10/20/rapidly-assessing-the-impact-of-hurricane-matthew-in-haiti.

———. 2018. "The World Bank in Haiti: Overview." Accessed 2 April 2018. http://www.worldbank.org/en/country/haiti/overview.

———. 2020. "GDP Growth (Annual %) – Haiti." Accessed 7 June 2020. https://www.worldbank.org/en/country/haiti/overview.

World Population. 2020. "Haiti Population." Accessed 6 June 2020. http://worldpopulationreview.com/countries/haiti-population.

World Statistical Data. 2019. "Port-au-Prince." Accessed 6 June 2020. https://populationstat.com/haiti/port-au-prince.

Zanotti, Laura. 2010. "Cacophonies of Aid, Failed State-Building, and NGOs in Haiti: Setting the Stage for Disaster, Envisioning the Future." *Third World Quarterly* 31 (5): 755–72.

Index